Being with Babies

Understanding and Responding to the Infants in Your Care

Beverly Kovach and Denise Da Ros-Voseles

Dedication

To my husband John, my two children Nicole and John, and my grandsons
Phoenix, Valin, and Roman
—Beverly Kovach
To my husband Charlie and my friend Paolo
—Denise Da Ros-Voseles

Acknowledgments

The authors wish to thank
◆ The parents of Little Learners' Lodge and Montessori of Mt. Pleasant, South
  Carolina for the use of their children's photos
◆ The staff of Little Learner's Lodge for their participation
◆ Photographers David and Nicole Vigliotti for their time and effort

I would like to thank my friend and mentor Magda Gerber for her wisdom,
patience, and acceptance of me. Her influence affected my personal and
professional relationships. I hold dear the memory of our long late-night
discussions.
I would also like to thank my Resources for Infant Educarers associates, especially
Carol Pinto, and my dearest and long-lasting colleague and friend Denise, whose
perseverance and commitment to this book have been remarkable. Thank you
also to caregivers of infants everywhere who form relationships with children and
their parents.

—Beverly Kovach

I would like to thank Mary Bates, who persuaded Beverly and me to provide
care for the very young child. This was the springboard that led Beverly to Magda
Gerber, and led me to an enduring interest and concern for the well-being of
infants and toddlers.
I would also like to thank my dear friend Beverly, whom I have watched develop
from an owner/operator of an infant/toddler center to a passionate, insightful
trainer who guides caregivers in best practices. Our ongoing collaboration has
helped connect me to infant and toddler issues over the years.

—Denise Da Ros-Voseles

Finally, we are grateful to our editor, Kathy Charner, editor-in-chief at Gryphon
House. Her adept editing and astute guidance is appreciated.

BEING WITH BABIES

Understanding and Responding to the Infants in Your Care

Best Practices for Caregivers

Beverly Kovach
Denise Da Ros-Voseles

© 2008 Beverly Kovach and Denise Da Ros-Voseles
Printed in the United States of America.

Published by Gryphon House, Inc.
10770 Columbia Pike, Suite 201, Silver Spring, MD 20901
301.595.9500; 301.595.0051 (fax); 800.638.0928 (toll-free)

Visit us on the web at www.gryphonhouse.com

Reprinted February 2010

Library of Congress Cataloging-in-Publication Data
Kovach, Beverly.
  Being with babies : understanding and responding to the infants in your care / Beverly Kovach and Denise Da Ros-Voseles.
      p. cm.
  Includes bibliographical references and index.
  ISBN 978-0-87659-062-1
  1. Infants--Care. 2. Child care workers. I. Da Ros-Voseles, Denise. II. Title.
  HQ778.5.K682 2008
  649'.1220284--dc22

                          2007050963

Bulk purchase
Gryphon House books are available for special premiums and sales promotions as well as for fund-raising use. Special editions or book excerpts also can be created to specification. For details, contact the Director of Marketing at Gryphon House.

Disclaimer
Gryphon House, Inc. and the authors cannot be held responsible for damage, mishap, or injury incurred during the use of or because of activities in this book. Appropriate and reasonable caution and adult supervision of children involved in activities and corresponding to the age and capability of each child involved, is recommended at all times. Do not leave children unattended at any time. Observe safety and caution at all times.

Every effort has been made to locate copyright and permission information.

Table of Contents

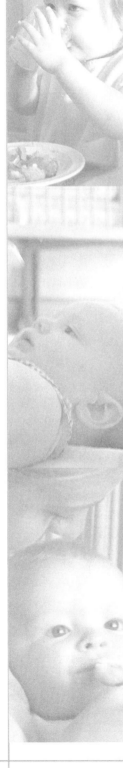

Preface

Letter from Beverly

Caring for babies has been a real birthing process and growth experience for me.

Originally, my interest was fueled by a mother whose child attended my child-care center. Mary "put a bug in my ear," so to speak, urging me to use some vacant space we had to start an infant center. When I reflect on that time, I see that Mary had the interest and desire, and I had the resources. I wasn't sure there was a need in the community, but I was willing to find out because I believed that babies didn't need much funding. Besides, what was so hard about taking care of babies? All they need is a crib, a bottle, and a little tender loving care. It seemed like an innocent request. Little did I  know! Because my emotional investment was minimal and time was a premium for me, I halfheartedly offered Mary the job. To my surprise, she accepted the offer and resigned from her position as a registered nurse.

Occasionally, I would ask Mary how she was doing, what the current enrollment was, and what income was being generated. After a year, Mary's part of the program was still afloat. Because of Mary's nudging, and after seeing the success of her hard work, I felt compelled to move the infant-care center in a more concrete direction.

Denise (administrator and co-founder of the center) and I seriously brainstormed about what we were going to do with babies. As professionals, we felt compelled to do something more than babysit young children. Denise suggested that we go listen to a speaker, Magda Gerber, who was considered the "guru" of caring for babies. So I said, "Let's go!" Denise and I attended a national conference the following month where Magda Gerber was speaking. I agreed to attend a session, but said to Denise, "Let's sit in the last row, get the handouts, and leave." When we arrived, there were only four seats, all in the front row. The small, dignified speaker in the gray suit standing by the podium welcomed us to the front row. As we sat down, I was reassured to see that there was an exit door on my left. Two significant things happened to me during Magda's session: I never received handouts, and I felt emotionally connected to her thoughts and words for the entire session. Magda's therapeutic voice captivated me. As she unraveled her philosophy about providing infant care by considering the baby's point of view, a light bulb went on. Everything she said made sense. Magda was a master at simplifying the complex. I was truly enchanted by her beliefs about how to understand babies. Our long-term friendship and mentorship was an energizing force that kept me on track with babies. For me, her gift for understanding was not just a philosophy about babies but a philosophy about living.

Learning about babies is a lifelong process that helps me understand myself and others. Trying to improve how to be with babies keeps my soul centered. The more I began to know and love Magda, the more involved I became with the infant program at our child-care center. As the years went by, I used the principles I learned in her parent-child classes to bring respectful caregiving to infants in group care. Over time, I experienced a personal metamorphosis. I was hooked! The quest of preserving the integrity of infant group care has become an obsession I treasure.

In this book, I hope to share this transformation with you through the eyes of the many caregivers who have helped me in my quest.

Beverly A Kovach

Letter from Denise

Prior to meeting Magda Gerber, Founder of Resources for Infant Educarers (RIE), I had little interest in infants. After all, I was the administrator of a large, well-known early childhood program for children from ages three through kindergarten, as well as an after-school program. My perspective changed when I attended one of Magda's training sessions. Her philosophy, based on respectful caregiving of infants, sounded so simple. Little did I know the ongoing effort it would take to bring this responsive caregiving to infants in center-based care.

Truthfully, I saw myself as a guiding light that would help Beverly to open up her mind about infant care. I suggested that we go to Magda's workshop at the National Association for the Education of Young Children (NAEYC) conference. After the conference, as Beverly became more involved in infant-care, I resumed my administrative function in the program. I let sleeping babies lie.

Later, when I was analyzing data on infant/toddler social and emotional functioning for my dissertation, I became aware of and developed an appreciation for the differences between Beverly's infant program and other centers. What I found was that, in Beverly's program, infants were more secure. They did not seek out the caregivers as much as children in other centers, and the infants were more content to explore and play on their own. The data suggested that the way infants' needs were met by the caregiver during physical care (diapering, eating, reading cues, and so on) resulted in babies seeking out their caregivers less at other times of the day than other babies in the study. The study validated that Magda's basic principles could be applied universally to other child-care centers, as well as other stages of child development.

After moving to another state, I found that the respectful caregiving of infants advocated by Magda Gerber was not a widespread aspect of group care. When observing possible sites for student placement, I was again reminded of the lack of quality infant care. I was concerned and frustrated by the lack of respectful infant caregiving.

Beverly and I continued to collaborate long-distance. Based on our experiences and observations, we did presentations and wrote articles about infants and toddlers. What we heard during our interactions with caregivers was their frustration about caregiving conditions in infant group care. These caregivers wanted to learn about how to provide more respectful infant care. Our experiences with the caregivers motivated Beverly and me to put in writing how babies affected our attitudes and our views in our professional practice. Our hope is that, in writing this book, we will meet the needs of the teachers and caregivers we met and influence others to care for babies in responsive and respectful ways.

Denise A. DaRos

Note: In this book, babies are defined as children from six weeks to 15 months old.

Introduction

This book is about the importance of caregivers and babies forming relationships through everyday caregiving interactions. The term caregiver is used throughout the book because it is the authors' belief and the belief of others (Eisler, 2007) that caring for babies is essential for a healthy society. Think about it: Without caring and caregiving, the long-term well-being of a culture is compromised.

Caregivers influence how babies think and interact as well as how they develop. The question is how will they make a difference? The authors believe that depends on how caregivers and infants react, respond, and relate to each other. Caregivers affect how babies view themselves and how they will relate to others in the future by the way they approach caring for and handling babies as well as responding to babies' needs.

We hope this book will provide beginning caregivers with a step-by-step guide to respectful practices, with explanations. More experienced caregivers may find individual chapters helpful when a situation or an issue arises. If you already instinctively involve babies in your caregiver practices, the content of this book will support why you provide care in certain ways. Or this book may prompt you to think more about your present caregiving practice. Teachers, trainers, and educators can use this book as a resource to highlight and support the importance of forming more secure attachments and relationships with babies. For example, scenarios provided in this book present concrete examples of respectful and responsive caregiving.

Chapter 1

A Challenge: Caring for Infants in a Child-Care Setting

Issue

Performing daily tasks while attending to the developmental needs of infants is a challenge in group care. In the rush to accomplish what needs to be done, it is easy to lose sight of how important it is to meet the needs of babies.

Rationale

Babies need many meaningful, focused, and unhurried experiences with caregivers throughout the day. These experiences help babies to feel valued and ensure that their needs will be met.

Goals

◆ To encourage meaningful experiences between babies and caregivers that create a special relationship
◆ To give focused attention to babies that communicates to them that they are valued

Doris opens the door to the infant room and immediately notes that the room needs cleaning and straightening. She mumbles to herself about what she needs to do to prepare the room for the children. Before she is able to straighten up the room, a mom enters with her six-month-old infant, Annie. Mom places Annie on a blanket and begins talking with Doris. When Mom leaves, Doris props Annie on her hip. Annie hears Doris's voice saying, "Now where did I put that broom? I have to find that broom." Annie rides around on Doris's hip. She gets a first-hand view of how Doris tidies the room.

Two parents enter with their babies. The parents begin to talk about the mayor's sister. Baby Annie looks confused. She hears noises and watches the different faces. The mothers settle their babies in the room before leaving. Doris warms up a bottle for one of the babies who is crying. Annie, still perched on Doris's hip hears, "I have to get some toys for you before I feed James." Annie bends with Doris as she empties the basket of toys on the floor. Doris puts Annie on the floor and surrounds her with toys. Doris retrieves crying James from the crib. Baby Annie screams in outrage.

The second caregiver, Latoya, enters the room, turns the radio to her favorite music station, and asks, "Why is Annie crying?" Doris says, "I don't know what is wrong with Annie. I have to feed James. Take Annie's temperature. She is out of sorts this morning. Maybe she is getting sick."

You've been there. You've seen this. You may have experienced the "I have to" syndrome. With the ideas and suggestions in this chapter and in this book, you, the caregiver, can figure out what needs to be done differently.

We can only guess how Annie feels about what is happening to her. And what is happening? While Annie's teacher is rushing around trying to get things done, Annie's needs are being ignored. Annie's teacher, Doris, is missing opportunities to connect and communicate directly with Annie. In addition, all the noise and chatter may make Annie feel confused and anxious. Maybe she feels frustrated, tired, or overwhelmed. Doris appears too busy to notice Annie's reactions to what is happening to her. Doris is ignoring Annie's feelings.

Doris's actions communicate many messages to Annie. What do Doris's actions say?

◆ She is unaware of the impact of her behavior on Annie.
◆ She draws conclusions about what Annie needs without connecting with Annie.
◆ She is unaware of Annie's reaction to what is happening.
◆ She talks about Annie as if she were not there.
◆ Her rushing may make Annie feel anxious and confused.

Doris is in the "I have to" mode. She feels like she has so much to do that she rushes about doing what she can. And because she is rushing, she fails to observe Annie's reactions, and she misses what is going on with Annie.

Doris also spent time talking with other adults. This compromises Annie's care. How (and why) did Doris forget her primary reason for being in the infant room? There may be many reasons. Maybe Doris is too task oriented. She may feel the stress of not having enough time, so she rushes to get her job done. By rushing, Doris gives Annie the message that she is unimportant, and she misses and ignores Annie's cues. When Doris hurries about doing what she thinks needs to be done she misses opportunities to develop a valuable relationship that will allow Annie to thrive. That can happen if Doris slows down, takes time, and puts Annie's care first.

Like Doris, many adults who work with babies feel they must be doing something in order to be a productive caregiver. Sometimes that means the signals from babies get ignored because the adults around them are too busy doing tasks. In addition, some adults believe babies are not yet able to understand what is happening. This belief can undermine what the baby needs because babies do communicate their needs with cues. When a caregiver assumes what a baby needs rather than responding to the baby's actions, this tells the baby that she is not valued because her cues were not understood. This, in turn, can lead to impersonal and inaccurate caregiving, in which the relationship between the caregiver and the baby are compromised.

What might help Doris respond to and communicate with baby Annie? What do you suppose Annie would ask from Doris? Annie wants Doris to look at her to see what she needs. Annie wants to say to Doris, "Look at me. I'm uncomfortable on your hip."

What could Doris do to help Annie understand that her needs are important?
- Slow down and observe how Annie is reacting. By observing the baby, Doris can be more accurate. Why is the baby crying? Is she wet? When did she last eat? Is she tired? Did something frighten her? Asking these questions helps Doris to think before responding to the baby.
- Talk to the baby about what she is about to do. When Doris tells the baby what she is going to do, she gives a signal or cue that something is about to happen. This cue allows the baby time to respond. When Doris speaks before acting, she helps Annie understand what is happening.
- Give undivided, uninterrupted attention when you are with the baby. When Doris is "fully there," it offers Annie time that is just hers. What better way to let Annie know she is special!

When a caregiver assumes what a baby needs rather than responding to the baby's actions, this tells the baby that she is not valued because her cues were not understood.

Following these simple suggestions affects how the baby feels about herself, and it helps you develop a more respectful and meaningful relationship between you and the baby in your care. Although these small steps are simple, they may not be easy to do.

Key Point

Your relationship with the babies in your care affects their development and learning. You are an important link to their well-being. Distractions, interruptions, and rushing take away from important valuable experiences and interactions between you and the babies.

Solutions

◆ Slow down and observe the baby before reacting.
◆ Give individual, focused attention when relating to the baby.
◆ Tell the baby what you are about to do before you do it.
◆ Minimize interruptions that add confusion and distract your focus on the babies.

Chapter 2
Authentic Caregiving

Issue

When your feelings and thoughts do not match your actions, you give babies mixed messages as you care for them. For example, telling a baby how important he is as you rush while changing his diaper gives the baby two different messages. Giving infants mixed messages confuses them, which is unsettling.

Rationale

Babies are keenly aware of and influenced by the people who care for them. Consequently, how caregivers act and interact with babies affects their development, especially their social and emotional development. When a caregiver's behavior reflects her true thoughts and emotions, her communication and interactions with babies is clear, and the relationship is authentic.

Goals

◆ To develop an awareness of your thoughts and emotions
◆ To understand the meaning of your thoughts and emotions
◆ To be true to yourself
◆ To nurture authentic caregiving with infants
◆ To realize that babies are aware of and sensitive to the behaviors and emotions of the people around them

These goals bring to mind the line "To thine own self be true" from Shakespeare's "Hamlet." Understanding and being true to yourself means that you know both your abilities and your limitations.

In addition, an important aspect about feelings is knowing when to act on them, and when not to act on them. For example, it is okay to *feel badly* when you've had a bad day, but it's not okay to *act badly* because you've had a bad day. Just because you had a flat tire on the way to work doesn't give you permission to take it out on others. When you are taking care of babies and you feel stressed, uptight, or out of sorts, do what you can to regain your composure, such as taking in a deep breath and slowly letting it out. If this does not work, request a short break to regroup so you have a fresh outlook. Being genuine doesn't mean you act on everything that you think and feel. It does mean that you identify and acknowledge your feelings.

SCENARIO

Marla was very friendly and all smiles in front of the parents of the children in her class. She was upbeat and talked sweetly about their "precious little darlings" until the parents left and the door was closed. Then her frustration and anger unfolded as the morning progressed. She would fuss at the babies when they didn't do as she expected. She often complained to the director, "I just can't take much more."

The director was confused by Marla's reaction because she knew how often the parents raved about Marla's patience and love of children. In front of the parents Marla was patient and loving toward the children. When Marla had to work all day with the children, her patience wore out. Marla's feelings and behavior gave the children mixed messages. Her interactions with the children when their parents were not present conveyed her true emotions. Marla suffered from job burnout. Her absenteeism increased and ultimately she left and went into a different field.

If Marla could have been true to her feelings (authentic), then what she said, felt, and did with the children would reflect the same meaning. In other words, she would have been authentic. When caregivers are being authentic, they are less likely to confuse babies (or anyone else) by giving them mixed messages.

There is value in being real and genuine when relating to babies. The primary reason is that babies absorb information from the world around them. They learn from the adults that they relate to and are sensitive to feelings that they are surrounded by. Babies are like barometers for the feelings they encounter in their surroundings. Babies often react to the behaviors and emotions they experience and observe in others.

Bonnie, a caregiver in the infant room, was on the floor with a small immobile baby when Maddie, a beginning walker, moved close to the baby. Bonnie said, "Maddie, be gentle," as she stroked the infant and then Maddie. As Bonnie began to get up to move the baby from the floor, Maddie gently touched the baby, stroking her gently while looking at Bonnie.

"We teach gentleness by showing gentleness" (Gerber, 1987). Some caregivers would have prevented Maddie from trying to touch a young baby. Bonnie wanted to give Maddie the positive message that gentle touching is allowed.

Because babies are keen observers of your behavior, you need to serve as models for them. Your behavior influences babies' learning, so be clear in your actions. Understanding your beliefs about the abilities of babies helps you to be clear in your actions. For instance, caregivers who believe babies can engage in learning opportunities will provide babies with experiences that help them understand what is happening. Bonnie, an infant caregiver, values infants relating to one another so she models gentleness for the older infants to observe. She believes that it's okay for babies to respond to each other socially. Bonnie clearly defines her beliefs by her actions toward the babies. Authentic caregiving is when you believe in what you do and you do what you believe.

Authentic caregiving is when you believe in what you do and you do what you believe.

Consider the experience of a trainer who told teachers in a group care setting that lap bottle-feeding was important. The trainer's rule was that all bottle-fed babies were to be fed in the lap of a caregiver. While the trainer was on site, she saw teachers giving babies their bottles while holding the babies in their laps. When the trainer returned unannounced, she saw babies being fed with their bottles propped. The caregivers were embarrassed, and the trainer was discouraged. What was the underlying problem? Looking back, it was the trainer, not the caregivers, who believed that it was important that the babies be held when bottle-feeding. The teachers were following one set of rules when the trainer was on-site and another set when the trainer was off-site. This can happen when the caregivers do not believe the same thing the trainer believes. The caregivers were appeasing the trainer and obviously didn't believe that it did make a difference to hold babies while bottle-feeding. This was a powerful lesson for the trainer. She began to rethink the best way to approach caregiver training. She learned that she must begin any training by asking caregivers what they believed. Allowing caregivers to examine their beliefs is a great starting point for learning new ways of acting and interacting with babies.

Believe in what you do and do what you believe. To be authentic means to be true to your beliefs rather than do something to please others. However, remaining authentic also means you are willing to stay open to new ideas and information and expand your beliefs based on what you see happening with babies. You should not have to sacrifice or compromise your beliefs. Your own readiness is your guide to change.

Authentic Responses in Everyday Situations

Understanding yourself is the first step toward understanding babies. It is essential in forming relationships. Being genuine and "real" influences how you feel about yourself. When you are comfortable with yourself, you do not have to play a role for others. You can feel and be who you are. Knowing who you are as a caregiver and accepting who you are influences your care with babies. How can you, as a caregiver, work on becoming authentic with the babies you care for?

◆ Stay interested in who a baby is as an individual.

Babies on their backs have opportunities to watch and play with their hands.

Watching three-month-old Danella notice and play with her hands and fingers was interesting to her caregiver, Consella. She was amazed at how calm and focused Danella remained as she manipulated her fingers. Consella noticed each time she put Danella on her back; she would begin her hand play. Consella watched how much Danella enjoyed playing with her hands and provided many opportunities for her to be on her back. Consella's observation of and interest in Danella's interests and responses gave Consella valuable information about Danella's preferences.

◆ Respect the babies' different temperaments and unique traits.

Adrielle knew six-month-old Abby cried for a few minutes before falling to sleep, whereas four-month-old Noah often drifted off while playing. Adrielle reassured Abby it was time for her to rest and placed Noah in his bed before he closed his eyes. Adrielle understood the babies' different and unique temperaments, which helped her to give sensitive care to each child.

◆ Accept and allow babies to express their positive and negative feelings.

A perfect example of allowing infants to express their feelings was 10-month-old Matthew, who willingly participated in having his picture taken by photographers. When it was time for Matthew to pose for his school pictures, hiscaregiver was surprised by his loud cries of distress. Matthew's cries were the result of his honest response to a new situation and an unknown photographer. Typically, babies experience stranger anxiety between 8–10 months of age. Mathew's fear was a natural response to a stranger. Although this may be a trying situation for both the baby and caregiver, adults need to accept and be sensitive to the baby's authentic feelings and response to strangers. Babies are not capable of being dishonest. They can be a model to us to stay on a true path with ourselves.

◆ Put away notions about how you want the baby to be.

Anna Grace, a shy and reserved baby, did not display many behaviors or cues to engage the adults who cared for her. Instead, Anna Grace preferred to stay involved in objects and toys available to her in the playroom. When picked up or touched by caregivers, Anna Grace would watchfully observe the caregivers without demonstrating much affect or response. This bothered her caregiver, Lucinda, who wanted to reach out and help Anna Grace to be more friendly and expressive. Lucinda felt Anna Grace lacked emotion. She would often try to get Anna Grace to behave more like Luke who giggled and kicked excitedly when picked up. Lucinda's disappointment increased, resulting in her approaching Anna Grace less. Maybe Lucinda could have been more sensitive to Anna Grace's slow-to-warm-up temperament by quietly sitting near her to give Anna Grace more time without placing any expectations (demands) on her. Giving more time to Anna Grace may have provided her with the opportunity to be ready to engage with Lucinda.

During your career, you might work in a center where your philosophy of how things need to be does not match the philosophy of the workplace. If this is true, you may be happier choosing to work in a setting that is more compatible with your philosophy.

This baby enjoys sitting quietly, inspecting a toy.

An administrator who was interviewing a prospective employee was curious why this caregiver was leaving the center where she was working after 11 years. The administrator asked, "Why are you changing now?" The employee responded, "I don't like what they do with the babies. I don't believe in their approach to babies, and I think I would be happier someplace else." Obviously, this caregiver had enough self-esteem, felt trapped where she was working, and wanted to see what was available elsewhere. She also had definite ideas about what needed to be done with babies, or she wouldn't be looking for a different job.

SCENARIO

"To thine own self be true" may mean finding employment elsewhere. No caregiver should be expected to compromise what she feels is important when giving care to babies. And, all caregivers who work with babies have the right to available resources (advocates, mentors, and trainers) that support and challenge new thinking.

Remember, "Minds are like parachutes. They only function when they are open." (Dewar, 1998, p. 40)

Key Point

Understanding what you believe will give you insight into why and how you respond to babies and workplace situations. If you believe in what you do, then you will be able to be true to yourself. Being open and willing to try new ideas while retaining your sense of self is a necessary part of your professional growth.

Solutions

- Reflect on your core beliefs about giving care to babies.
- Identify and understand your feelings and thoughts before reacting.
- Authentic caregiving requires that you believe in what you do and do what you believe with babies.
- As you care for babies, be mindful about their capabilities and be open to changing your beliefs based on what you see happening with babies.

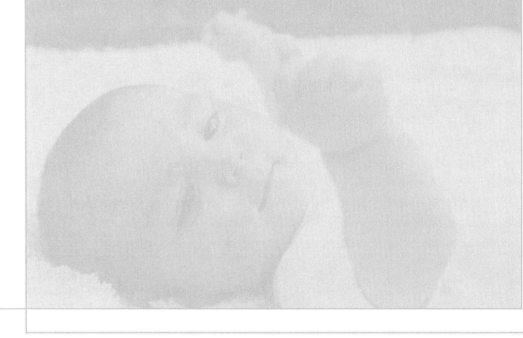

Chapter 3

Believing That Babies Are Capable

Issue

When you believe that babies are helpless, you are likely to do more for them than they need. This sets up a cycle of dependency. When babies are given opportunities to demonstrate their capabilities, the notion of the babies as an "empty vessel" becomes a myth.

Rationale

When you give babies opportunities to demonstrate their capabilities, it is impossible to view babies as an "empty vessel," a common myth. Repeated experiences with babies will help you learn and understand babies' abilities. These experiences will influence what you believe babies are capable of doing and how you behave when caring for babies.

Goals

- ◆ To examine your existing beliefs about babies
- ◆ To understand how your beliefs affect your attitudes and behaviors with babies
- ◆ To have an open mind about having experiences with babies that provide insights that challenge your existing beliefs
- ◆ To develop an awareness of the effect of your behavior on babies and their abilities

You *do* make a difference for each baby you have a relationship with. What you do today with babies in your care makes a difference in their lives tomorrow. You actually influence who babies will eventually become (Gonzalez-Mena & Eyer, 2004; National Scientific Council of the Developing Child, 2004).

Developing a strong belief about your work and its importance, and the type of care you give, requires a commitment on your part. Because our culture does not often value babies as individuals, the important work you do with babies is often unnoticed or unappreciated. It is important to begin to learn the best way to relate with babies. This includes knowing and understanding what babies are capable of doing.

SCENARIO

Beverly, an infant caregiver, believed spending quality time during caregiving times, such as diapering and feeding, allowed her to form a bond with the babies in her care. Beverly felt that paying attention to each baby in this way gave the babies a strong message that they were important.

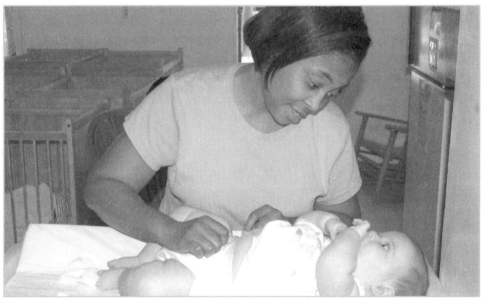

When the caregiver pays full attention to the baby, the baby receives the message that she is valued.

When she was diapering or feeding 11-month-old Julia, Beverly used slow movements and gave her full attention to infant Julia. This way of being with Julia was as gratifying to her as she hoped it would be for Julia. Beverly often was amazed at how alert Julia became when she began to talk to her about what Beverly was doing or what was happening. One day as Beverly was changing Julia's diaper, she asked Julia to lift, and the baby actually lifted up her bottom. Needless to say, Beverly was delighted that the baby was able to understand and do what Beverly had asked. When given the opportunity to be a part of her care, Julia was able to show she could participate. This reinforced Beverly's belief that her sensitive-care relationship made a positive difference.

Many factors determine the type of care you give babies. These factors include how you were raised, your observations and perceptions, what you think babies can do, the culture you belong to, and experiences you have with babies.

SCENARIO

Johanna has been working in the infant room for about two months. Before coming to the center, she had no previous experience with babies. Until she started working with infants, Johanna believed babies were fragile and helpless. In the beginning, she was afraid to pick up and hold a baby for fear she might hurt the baby. As days went on, a more experienced caregiver helped Johanna be less anxious and fearful around the babies. She learned through repeated exposure that babies are not as fragile as she thought. She observed daily how babies' movements were able to get them where they wanted to go.

Through her experiences with babies, Johanna became more knowledgeable and understanding about how babies behave. Her experiences helped her change her beliefs about babies. Johanna's past beliefs became less of an influence. Her new beliefs changed her thinking and her behavior.

Some popular myths about babies are that babies are helpless, that they do not know anything yet, and that they are "empty vessels" that need to be filled. If you show babies through your actions that you believe these myths are true, they become more dependent. For example, if you believe babies are helpless, you are apt to do more for the baby than is needed. Doing more leaves little room for the baby to participate in his or her care. Your attitudes influence babies' self-concept and self-worth.

There is another popular belief that can influence the care you give to babies. For instance, if you believe that babies would receive better care at home from their parents, then it is easy to adapt the "poor thing attitude" with the baby who is in group care. Some caregivers believe that babies in group care don't get enough mom (or dad) because mom (or dad) is at work. When caregivers develop the "poor thing attitude," they often support over-doing, over-checking, and over-stimulating the baby. The caregiver may try to give more than is needed, which can make babies too dependent.

To add to the confusion, there are experts offering different philosophies on what is best for babies. If you've ever browsed the self-help aisle of a book store, you have seen a good example of this. There are so many sources saying different things, it is easy to be confused about what is really best for babies. To simplify all this advice, the key element to keep in mind when caring for babies is that relationships are primary to infant health, especially in the early years of life.

The key element to keep in mind when caring for babies is that relationships are primary to infant health, especially in the early years of life.

In addition to the key element of understanding that relationships are crucial to the well-being and development of babies, *observation* is the other key element. By observing babies, they can tell us what they need. Each baby is different and has different needs. Much of what you do needs to rely on your observation and your interpretation of what you see happening with that particular baby. It takes time and patience to learn what works and doesn't work for each baby.

SCENARIO

Gloria came off the playground with 11-month-old Phoenix, a beginning walker, saying he needed to eat earlier than some of the other children in his group. "If he doesn't eat his lunch now, he will be cranky and tired and will not eat as well."

Gloria knew Phoenix's schedule and preferences. She was willing to make changes and concessions in order for Phoenix to be happy and meet his need for food. Her behavior is much different than a caregiver who tells the child to "Hush, lunch will be here soon," as she says to her coworker, "This baby is so spoiled! His parents always drop everything and give him what he wants."

Your attitudes and beliefs determine how you develop your caregiving practice with babies. The amount of time you spend trying to understand each baby will affect the type of care you give and the attitude the babies develop about their worth. In today's society, raising a child is an enormous and complex task. You can make a difference, especially when you sort out what you believe and develop a philosophy of care that honors your belief and the abilities of the babies in your care.

Make a difference by trying to develop habits that influence what you believe. Do this by remembering to:
◆ Quietly observe the baby in different settings and at different times.
◆ Watch one specific thing the baby is doing (for example, watch how he moves or how he plays with a toy).

Babies can focus on objects and people in their environment. They can also manipulate objects.

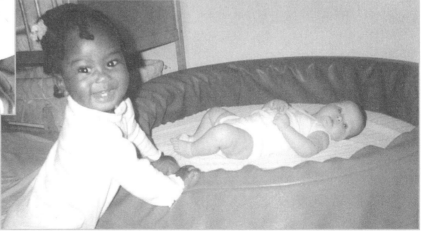

- Talk with the baby about what is happening between you and the baby, and wait for the baby's response.
- Slow down your actions so the baby will have time to respond to you during down times when neither you nor the baby needs something.
- Watch and appreciate what the baby is doing at different times throughout the day.

These measures will help to expand your view and broaden your insights about babies and their abilities. Your beliefs determine how you respond to babies. You make a difference. The difference is in the type of relationship you chose to have with each of the babies you relate to.

Key Point

Your attitude and beliefs affect what you do with babies. Knowing what you believe babies are capable of doing is important because it affects the type and quality of care you provide to babies. Through repeated experiences with babies, you gain knowledge that may challenge your existing beliefs. Your beliefs influence opportunities you provide for the baby to demonstrate his or her abilities.

Solutions

- Examine your existing beliefs about babies.
- Rely on observation to help you gain understanding and insight into each baby.
- Determine how your beliefs affect the type of experiences and care you give babies.
- Decide whether your care supports the baby's capabilities.
- Be open to re-evaluate your beliefs and how they influence your relationship with babies.
- Adjust your beliefs based on new insights.

Chapter 4

Trial and Error: The Way Capable Babies Learn

Issue

Caregivers play an important role in helping infants develop their abilities. You provide opportunities for babies to explore and discover safely as they develop their skills.

Rationale

All babies have certain capabilities in different stages of development. Your attitude about the abilities of babies and your willingness to let babies experience through trial and error are key factors that either encourage or discourage opportunities for babies to relate in their world.

Goals

- ◆ To provide babies opportunities to develop skills through trial and error
- ◆ To accept the babies' need to explore
- ◆ To support babies' efforts to choose objects that interest them
- ◆ To observe babies' actions
- ◆ To support babies' competence

Babies are more capable then most adults believe. Babies spend a lot of time and much effort as they try to accomplish a task over and over again. But, popular belief continues to portray babies as helpless human beings that rely on the adult for survival and existence (Kallo & Balog, 2005; Lally, 1995).

In some ways, babies are not totally capable. For example, babies are not able to prepare their own bottles for feeding. In other ways, however, babies are capable. For instance, babies cry when they are hungry. It is their way of letting you, their caregiver, know they need nourishment.

You may be surprised by the things that capture a baby's attention.

When you watch babies, you can begin to understand what they are trying to tell you by their behavior and the signals they give you. You get to know, understand, and appreciate what each baby can do, and that each baby is competent and responsible for his or her development. Your experiences with babies provide rich information to help you know and understand who they are and what they are capable of doing.

SCENARIO

When Marlene was beginning to change nine-month-old Elise's diaper at the changing table, she noticed Elise trying to take off the tabs on her diaper. Marlene responded by waiting and saying, "Elise, I see you are trying to be helpful with your diaper change." Marlene was quite amazed when Elise was successful at opening the tabs from both sides of her diaper.

Spending time with babies provides valuable information. Over time, this information will help you interpret and understand babies' cues. Observing and understanding babies takes time and commitment. You play a vital role in allowing the babies to experience their abilities. As a caregiver, you are part of the baby's world. What you do is part of what the baby learns. You influence the baby through your actions with them. Your attitude affects the way in which the baby can develop. The baby relies on you for opportunities to actively experience her abilities. It is important for you, as a caregiver, to support and respond to the baby's initiation and desires during his or her exploration.

When given the opportunity, babies can participate in their care.

SCENARIO

When 12-month-old Charlie was able to sit up, the caregiver placed him at the small table and chair for his feeding. She gave Charlie a small spoon and unbreakable juice glass. The caregiver sat across from the baby as she fed him. With spoon in hand, Charlie successfully used the spoon to put the food in his mouth. For the first time, he grasped the glass to sip milk. The caregiver was amazed by Charlie's ability to feed himself and sip from a glass. It had never dawned on her that Charlie possessed these feeding skills.

Babies learn by doing, through trial and error. Allowing babies to try to do things for themselves, with as little interference as possible, supports their development. You can reinforce their learning and development by simply allowing babies to accomplish small tasks. Have you ever noticed how often babies are carried in and out of a room? Opening the door and waiting might be all that is required for the baby to experience an adventure.

Babies explore and learn about objects through trial and error.

At one center, the caregivers' attitude provided daily opportunities for babies to do as much as they can on their own, with little assistance from caregivers. What does this look like in the everyday life of babies in a group setting? An example of this is a caregiver bending down to the eye level of a mobile infant who is moving very close to the door that opened into the playroom and asking Megan, "Do you want to go in this play space?" as she opened the door. Megan slowly crawled through the door and proceeded up the climbing structure. It seemed so natural for the caregiver to allow the baby to initiate a choice on her own.

Beliefs about babies being helpless often get in the way of allowing babies to experience their competence. It may be simpler to do these tasks yourself rather than to allow the baby's own efforts to unfold. But, consider how you can respond to and, therefore, influence babies' abilities to try to do something. Babies provide information about themselves through their actions in their environment. You can encourage a baby's capability by allowing choice to be part of the baby's experience. Through choice, the baby can develop preferences as he or she chooses the preferred object. By placing objects near the baby, he or she can grasp his or her choice. This gives the baby the opportunity to develop his or her abilities. When babies are given permission to initiate actions and explore their environment, they develop their abilities through the trial and error of their experiences. These trial-and-error experiences are what help babies learn how things work.

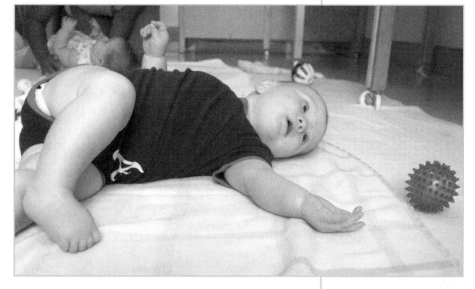

Placing objects near the baby allows him to choose what he wants to grasp.

Sometimes the obvious gets overlooked. Allowing babies to do and be all they can at their particular stage of development may seem simple and obvious. As a caregiver, you have the most influence on what the babies will be allowed to do and try. When you support the baby's ability to try, he or she learns and experiences what he or she can and can't do. Through trial and error, babies develop their own skills and abilities, but as the adult, you need to understand that the babies need these experiences to learn and develop skills. By giving the babies the opportunity to try, you make the difference in their development.

Key Point

Babies become competent when you allow them to do as much as they can on their own. You need to allow babies to discover what they can do and experience their environment through trial and error.

Solutions

◆ Refrain from doing more for babies than needed.
◆ Allow babies to choose objects that interest them.
◆ Observe babies' behaviors to understand their preferences.
◆ Enjoy babies' ability to relate to their world.
◆ Allow babies to have trial-and-error learning experiences.

Chapter 5

Primary Caregiving

Issue

Babies need to be "in" a special relationship with significant adults who respect and know them in order to thrive physically, emotionally, and cognitively. When you have a mutually satisfying relationship with babies in your care, trust, respect, and understanding develops.

Rationale

Primary care is a special cooperative relationship between you and the babies in your care that is introduced and maintained during caregiving times. Babies who are in a primary care relationship with an adult form secure attachments, freely explore their environment, and develop a sense of security that their needs will be met by someone who knows them well. Primary care times can be joyful learning opportunities for both you and the babies in your care.

Goals

- ◆ To develop and maintain a special relationship with each baby in your care that fosters mutual trust and understanding
- ◆ To provide ample opportunities for thoughts, feelings, and behaviors to be expressed in and during the primary care relationship

Thirteen-month-old Asami smiled enthusiastically as she saw her caregiver, Renata, enter the infant room. Renata noticed Asami smiling at her as she made eye contact. Renata greeted Asami as she moved toward her, bending down with a warm "Hello, I'm glad to see you today." Asami quickly crawled to sit in her special friend's lap and gave Renata a big hug. "Thank you for the hug," said Renata as she took Asami's hands gently in hers. "I missed you too." Noting Asami looking toward the refrigerator, Renata said, "You seem ready for your glass of milk." Asami stood up, took Renata's hand, and moved toward the refrigerator. She watched patiently as Renata poured milk into her glass, and then asked Asami if she was ready to sit at the table. Asami sat on her stool and looked at Renata as if asking Renata to sit next to her. Renata sat down saying, "I was just about to come over when I saw you looking

at me." Once Asami was finished, Renata got Asami's favorite book as Asami toddled to their quiet corner. They sat together looking and pointing at the pictures. Asami seemed pleased that Renata remembered to bring her favorite book to their special time together.

The above scenario is an example that clearly shows Asami and Renata have a special relationship. Their relationship is based on knowing, caring, understanding, and enjoying each other. They are tuned in to one another and the dialogue between them is special. This type of relation-based care can occur in infant care centers when there is a primary caregiver. This primary person enters into a relationship with a small group of babies and gives individual time and attention to these babies especially during caregiving times.

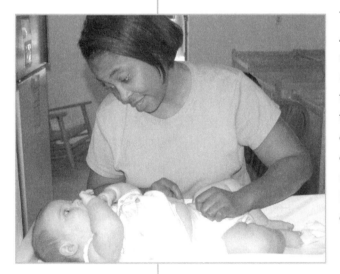

Diapering is a caregiving routine that offers an opportunity for a caregiver and a baby to build and maintain their relationship.

Key Point

Primary care is essential for babies to thrive developmentally and can be mutually satisfying and enjoyable for you and for babies. Through primary care, babies learn their needs will be met by a caring and sensitive caregiver who understands them as unique individuals. Primary care is most successful in centers when the ratio of babies to caregiver does not exceed four babies to one caregiver. One way a caregiver can accomplish some aspects of primary care is to verbally acknowledge a baby who expresses a need when the caregiver is busy with another baby by saying, "I heard you and I will be with you as soon as I'm done helping Jane." Once babies learn that waiting has a benefit (for example, their needs will be met), babies will begin to understand and will be able to wait better. During quiet times in the infant room, build relationships with babies who are awake and available.

Solutions

◆ Caregivers and babies need to be in a relationship together that fosters trust and mutual understanding.
◆ Each baby needs a primary person that knows and understands his or her needs, preferences, and cues.
◆ Keep group size small and developmentally compatible.
◆ Use caregiving routines to learn about and meet the physical and emotional needs of babies.

Chapter 6

The Three Rs: Respectful, Responsive, And Reciprocal Caregiving

Issue

Respectful, responsive, and reciprocal care needs to be a part of everyday practice with babies in group settings. Being respectful to babies includes being sensitive to the needs of babies by following important cues that help you understand what they need. Distractions and interruptions can easily undermine the care process in child-care settings. These interruptions prevent caregivers from remaining focused and present with the baby.

Rationale

When caregivers react in sensitive, responsive ways to meet each baby's individual needs the baby feels worthwhile and valued. Watching, asking, adapting, talking, and responding are key behaviors that make up responsive care. This means waiting for responses by babies and including that response in the next action. This reinforces responsiveness in caregiving practice.

Goals

◆ To respect each baby as a valued individual
◆ To observe baby's cues and respond based on sensitive observation
◆ To be responsive and include the baby's reaction in your next behavior
◆ To use behaviors that reinforce respectful, responsive, and reciprocal care for babies

Caregivers know how difficult it is to meet the needs of babies while in group care. There are several reasons for this problem: caregivers are in short supply, there are many interruptions throughout the day that distract the care processes, and resources and training for caregivers may not always be available. But, the goal should continue to be to try to provide responsive and respectful care for babies.

Louisa picked up four-month-old Roman from his bed and noticed he had a soiled diaper. While she was interacting with Roman as she changed his diaper, her supervisor came over to the diaper change area and said, "Louisa, do you have anything to add for the staff meeting tomorrow?" Louisa looked up momentarily and then said, "I'm with Roman now. I can talk with you when I'm done taking care of him."

Louisa continued to maintain full concentration and presence during her diapering of Roman even when her supervisor interrupted her interactions as she changed Roman. Louisa believed that Roman deserved her full attention during their care process together. Maintaining her focus and presence to Roman demonstrated her belief in respectful and responsive caregiving relationships. What a great way to let Roman know he is valued and respected!

When one person respects another it means to hold and honor that person in the highest regard. Babies in your care need to be treated with respect and valued as individuals. This means that you communicate with them in responsive ways. When you are responsive, you are sensitively involved in the process with the baby from the time you pick up the baby to care for him or her until the baby's caregiving needs are met. You let the baby know that his cues and behaviors are heard. The information the baby gives you through his cues and behaviors is what you use to respond to him, thereby telling him that you understand what he needs. This reciprocal care is the way to tell infants that they are respected.

Babies can participate in their care process.

In an article published by Kovach and Da Ros (1998), the authors stated several factors that are key to responsive group care:

◆ Babies need opportunities for peaceful caregiving times with adults as well as time alone to explore.

◆ Babies need to participate in the caregiving process.

◆ Babies need opportunities for choice.

Babies need time to figure out how to solve their problems and struggles.

- Babies need to move freely and in a safe environment.
- Babies need sensitive, individualized, predictable routines with a significant adult.
- Babies need interactions with other babies who are at the same stage of development.
- Babies' physical needs are based on their own body's schedule, not a room schedule.
- Babies' cues need to be observed to understand what is best for them at a given time.
- Babies need time to experience how to solve their problems and struggles.

Respectful and responsive caregiving, which is not an easy task to accomplish in group care, develops trust and mutual satisfaction between you and the infant. "Watching, asking, and adapting are the tools of responsive caregiving" (Lally, Griffin, Fenichel, Segal, Szanton, & Weissbourd, 1995). Babies in group care thrive when, as part of their relationship with their caregiver, they are included in their caregiving process by a responsive and emotionally involved adult.

Key Point

Babies thrive in group care when you relate to their needs in respectful and responsive ways. When you acknowledge and enter into a responsive relationship to meet the needs of babies, they feel valued and understood.

Solutions

- Respond to babies' cues based on their needs.
- Watch, ask, and adapt to provide responsive and respectful care.
- Avoid interruptions and distractions that take away from the caregiving process with babies.
- Stay emotionally involved with the babies in your care.

Chapter 7

Stop and Look: The Key to Observation

Issue

Look first and act second. Observation helps you eliminate what you think the baby is trying to communicate. It is easy to make incorrect assumptions when you do not let yourself take enough time to see what is happening.

Rationale

Observation is a valuable tool that helps you learn, appreciate, and understand babies. It is a way to check in with a baby to see how he or she is doing and to decide if the baby needs something or is content for the time being.

Goals

◆ To appreciate each individual baby's unique way of expressing himself or herself

◆ To understand each baby's way of giving important cues about his or her needs and wants

◆ To appreciate and enjoy each baby's stage of development; what he or she can do, and what he or she is not yet ready to do, respecting each child's individual readiness

A wise practitioner once said, "Observe more and do less" (Gerber & Johnson, 1998). When 12-month-old Roman came upon a small decline in the flooring, the caregiver Sophia observed how he was able to maintain his balance while moving down from the step. Sophia's observation enabled her to wait instead of rushing to help. Observing more and doing less is a skill that comes with practice. Through observation, caregivers can understand babies and how to meet their needs. Because babies communicate a lot of information nonverbally, you must be able to read the baby's cues to understand what the baby is trying to say. Through careful observation, you will be able to gather information about each baby. Observation is the key to understanding.

Observation is a skill that takes time and practice.

Observing is a skill that takes practice. Observation should always be the first step before you react to what is happening. This means that you need to stop thinking about yourself and stop projecting your feelings onto what you see. Consider the following example involving a caregiver who was insensitive in her observation.

SCENARIO

Amelia is feeding five-month-old Nasser. He often turns away from his bottle and gazes around the room before returning to be fed. This happens several times, which to Amelia, indicates he is no longer hungry. Despite the bottle being only half full, she attempts to put the baby down to play. Nasser begins to cry. Amelia wonders what to do next.

Had Amelia followed Nasser's gaze, she would have noticed that he was distracted and was looking at a bright red-and-blue beach ball. Being a five-month-old, Nasser is increasingly interested in the world around him and how it works. He was intrigued by the beach ball and turned his eyes away from the caregiver, who was trying to feed him. Had Amelia been more keenly observant and waited patiently, Nasser might have returned to his bottle. Maybe Amelia could have engaged Nasser to return to their feeding relationship. Cues can be subtle. When you develop keen observation skills, you are more apt to notice these subtle cues. The three essential things to remember about observing are to stop, look, and listen.

Stop

Observation is an art that requires time. To observe, you first have to slow down. Take a few minutes out of your busy day. Go to the corner of your infant room. Quietly look around. It can be difficult to stop and do nothing but observe. It can be hard to take time to observe babies, but if you make yourself stop, look, and listen for a few minutes, you will develop better observation skills. Stopping helps you to look and see what is happening.

On a tour for parents, a director of an infant program relayed how the caregiver sits and watches the babies as they play on the floor. One parent asked, "Why is she [referring to the caregiver] just sitting there? Shouldn't she be doing something?" The director patiently explained, "This caregiver is observing the babies. She is the eyes and ears for these babies. Using the information she has gained through observation, she interprets what babies are trying to communicate and helps them when they need something," explained the director. It is important for parents to understand how sensitive observation helps caregivers to understand and respond to babies' needs.

Look

To look means to see what is there without judging or projecting. Babies are excellent observers. Maybe that is because they have few worries. To be successful at observing you need to "empty your head" of thoughts that do not pertain to the task at hand. Take a deep breath and let it out. Let the worries in your life go out with the second deep breath. Now you are ready to see the baby. The following exercise will help you to develop a peacefulness that is needed for you to be in the here and now.

Consider the following when observing babies:
◆ Slow down.
◆ Quiet and calm your body.
◆ Empty your head.
◆ Forget about yourself.
◆ Stay in the present; forget about the past or future.
◆ Go to a quiet area and blend into the wall (be like a fly on the wall).
◆ Select one baby to watch.
◆ Do this every day for five minutes.
◆ Say out loud what you see; this reinforces your observation.
◆ Talk to a coworker about your observations.

Understanding what babies are trying to communicate means you must stop, look, and listen to try to figure out the baby's message. Observation requires interest, discipline, and practice. The more often you practice observing babies, the more accurate your efforts will be.

Understanding what babies are trying to communicate means you must stop, look, and listen to try to figure out the baby's message.

Listen

Listen with your ears and mind open. Develop a sense of *really* hearing. Step back and try to understand what the baby is trying to communicate and say by his or her vocalization. All coos, utterances, and sounds have meanings. Are the sounds happy, sad, tired, or frustrated? Do the sounds give you the message that he or she is content or dissatisfied? The sensations you feel from baby's sounds give valuable information about how he or she feels and his or her state of well-being.

Key Point

When you take time to observe babies, you gain valuable information that will help you understand and accurately meet the needs of babies. Babies give cues that can be observed. By slowing down and taking time to watch babies, you will better understand what they are trying to communicate. Obtaining information about babies requires observing with an open mind. As you observe babies, you will be better able to respond to cues from babies.

Solutions

◆ Use observation as a valuable tool to know and understand each baby in your care.
◆ Give yourself time each day to practice observing babies.
◆ Take time to stop, slow down, and watch what is happening with babies in the "here and now."
◆ Use all your senses to help determine babies' state of well-being.

Chapter 8

Giving Time: The Art of Slowing Down

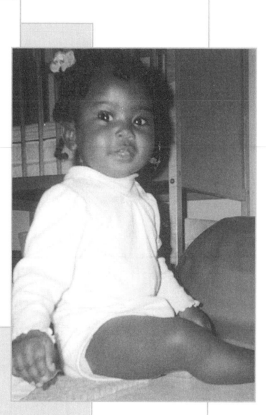

Issue

When you slow down and stop rushing through the day, you can give babies your time and attention, which is what you both need to develop and maintain your relationships with the babies in your care. Making a commitment to take time to relate with babies means that you need to slow down and stay in the here and now. Rushing through daily tasks makes it impossible to give quality time to babies.

Rationale

As a caregiver, you can make a difference in the lives of babies in your care when you slow down and give them your undivided attention. To do this, you need to make a commitment to be emotionally present with the babies in your care.

Goals

- To sit and give "wants nothing" time to enjoy the baby—this is time spent with the baby when there is no set plan or agenda except to listen and enjoy being with the baby
- To slow down, become peaceful, and stay in the present moment
- To be emotionally present with the babies in your care
- To set a certain time of the day to touch base with each baby in your care

What is the one thing that you can give someone that doesn't cost money and that says to them, "You are very special"? Time! Time spent listening, responding, and trying to understand. Hurrying is the enemy of time. Where does rushing take us: to the next task on our to-do list. It becomes a vicious circle. If you remove the pressure and the presence of the clock from the infant room, it might help you slow down and give you a chance to watch and appreciate the babies. Giving time to the babies in your care is your way of saying that you feel they are special.

What is the best way to give babies your time? There is a magic formula for giving babies time: making the commitment + emptying your head + staying in the present + keeping a slow, calm pace + spending quality here-and-now time = giving time.

Magda Gerber, an infant and toddler expert, urged teachers to "enjoy more and do less," while acknowledging that this is not an easy task. Magda often wove this theme into her Resources for Infant Educarers (RIE) infant-toddler course. Respect is the foundation for her RIE philosophy, with basic principles to support that respect. Some of her basic principles include trusting the child to be an initiator and explorer, providing a physically safe and cognitively challenging environment, and offering babies time for uninterrupted play (see *Your Self-Confident Baby* by Gerber & Johnson [1998] for a more thorough explanation).

Take time to stop, slow down, and watch what is happening with babies in the "here and now."

Mr. Rogers, a well-known child advocate and television personality, once said, "You need patience to wait through the natural silence of life" (Rogers, 1998). Both Magda Gerber and Mr. Rogers are reminding us to slow down and appreciate the simplicity of life. In order to "unhurry" a child, you need to "unhurry" yourself and slow down. Only then, can you really enjoy and appreciate the time you have with the babies in your care.

Sitting back and watching what babies do gives you a chance to see the wonders of development unfold, but this takes practice. One of the most difficult tasks reported by caregivers is monitoring babies during their play. As babies move and explore, it is hard to stay alert and responsive. It is easy for the mind to wander. Also, learning to appreciate babies' behaviors takes sensitive observation and time.

This baby enjoys sitting quietly, inspecting a toy.

Julia, a fairly new employee, was sitting in the playroom of a mobile infant room propped against the wall, looking out the window. She appeared quite involved in her personal thoughts. Five babies were playing nearby. Amelia, an 11-month-old, was playing on a nearby gross-motor structure. She kept hesitating to crawl down the ramp and would look over at Julia trying to get her attention, but to no avail.

When Adrielle, the lead teacher in this center-based facility, brought 13-month-old Ashley into the playroom after her nap, Julia still continued her daydreaming. Adrielle put Ashley down and asked Julia if any of the babies needed something. Julia responded with a smile, saying, "All the babies are fine." Although no baby was creating a fuss, were all the babies fine? How could Amelia have used Julie's support and presence? How could Julie have been more available to Amelia?

Often caregivers like Julie watch babies who are contently playing and slowly ease into a zoned-out state. When this happens, they miss valuable opportunities to be available to babies and to nurture their relationship together. When you take time to enjoy your relationship with the babies in your care, you are apt to appreciate the babies, who they are, and what they are able to do. This gives you insight and understanding about each baby's unique individuality. Your interest tells the babies that they are important and special. Giving time provides ample opportunity for each of you to get to know one another in a deeper and meaningful way. "Time in" together deepens your relationship and provides both you and the baby a better understanding of each other.

When you take time to enjoy your relationship with the babies in your care, you are apt to appreciate the babies, who they are, and what they are able to do.

Justine had a very busy week in the infant room with a new baby she was assigned. Getting to know and understand baby Mikel required a lot of time and effort on her part. It took a great deal of patience on the part of Justine to be able to read, respond to, and understand Mikel's cues. However, Justine's trial and error paid off as she began to understand Mikel's wants and needs. As the days went by, Justine realized how much she enjoyed being with Mikel now that she understood him better. Because their relationship deepened, Justine and Mikel found that they looked forward to their time together.

Giving your time to babies means you have to be emotionally present. To do this you need to slow yourself down and make a conscious effort to stay in the present moment. Giving of yourself is an art, one worth cultivating for your own sense of pleasure and satisfaction as well as for the babies.

Key Point

Giving time requires a commitment on your part to understand that you make a difference when you are emotionally present with babies. When you give babies quality time, you communicate to babies that they are valued and special.

Solutions

A caregiver enjoying the moment with a baby.

- ◆ Schedule special quality time in your day with each baby in your care.
- ◆ Decrease the number of tasks in your daily to-do list.
- ◆ Slow down and enjoy the present moment with the baby.
- ◆ Giving time requires you to stay emotionally present with the baby.

Chapter 9

Cues Are Clues

Issue

For babies to thrive and be content, caregivers must accurately read their cues. When babies have the opportunity to express their needs and preferences, their well-being is recognized and maintained.

Rationale

Caregivers need to trust babies' ability to make their needs known as they respond to cues from babies. These interactions—babies making their needs known and caregivers responding to them—help babies learn how to understand what their bodies say to them. Keen observation and persistence in trying to understand what is happening are valuable skills for caregivers to know.

Goals

- ◆ To accurately observe and understand babies' cues
- ◆ To understand what babies are trying to say with their cues
- ◆ To value babies' cues during caregiving routines
- ◆ To respond sensitively to babies' cues using daily experiences
- ◆ To help babies understand their likes and dislikes

Olivia is feeding seven-and-a-half-month-old Jeremiah in a bouncy seat. Jeremiah stops sucking at the bottle, Olivia jiggles the bottle and says, "Drink, it's good for you." Jeremiah tries to avoid the nipple as Olivia gently attempts to push the nipple into his mouth. "Please drink your formula because Allie is also hungry, and I need to feed her next." Olivia persists in trying to force Jeremiah to drink his bottle. She stops when he begins to cry loudly.

Grace, an eight-month-old, is sitting on a small stool at a small table. Iris, the caregiver, sits across from her. Her food and spoon are placed on the table for her to see. There is still food on her plate when Grace begins to turn her whole body away from the table. Iris asks, "Are you done eating your peas, Grace?" Grace stops and looks at Iris, who presents Grace with another spoonful of peas. Grace turns away from the peas. Iris says, "I see that you may be full." Iris puts down the spoon and asks Grace for her hands. Iris shows the baby the washcloth and says, "I need to wipe your hands." Grace tries to put her hand in the cloth. After Grace's hands are wiped, and her bib removed, Iris reaches out her hands and says, "Are you ready to go and play? I will take you to the playroom." Grace responds with outstretched arms.

These feeding scenarios give the babies two different messages. In the first, Olivia is responding to Jeremiah based on *her* needs. Jeremiah is being encouraged to drink a bottle he no longer wants. He tries to avoid the bottle. When Olivia insists Jeremiah drink his bottle, she ignores Jeremiah's cues, which are important signs of his desires and needs. When caregivers notice and respond to these cues, babies are more likely to have their needs met and to feel understood.

◆ Pay Attention to Babies' Cues

Cues signal what a baby prefers, and babies' preferences eventually define their needs and desires. Babies' cues are their way of saying what they need. When babies' cues are ignored, the message they receive is that what they want is not important, and that what their bodies are saying to them is not true. This may confuse the babies, who then learn to ignore what their bodies are telling them. As a result, babies may stop initiating cues. In Jeremiah's case, he learns not to trust what he feels his body needs.

It may be easy for you to forget or be insensitive to babies' wants and desires. You may not consider developmental milestones so your guesses might be inaccurate. To be more accurate, your guess needs to be based on observing babies' cues and relating to them with hands-on experiences. Knowing babies well enough to understand their preferences and individual needs enables you to understand what babies are saying by their cues.

Taking time to value each baby's individual desire is not easy to accomplish in center-based care. But, babies are happier and thrive when their cues are acknowledged and accurately interpreted. This is obvious in the scenario when Iris included the baby's reaction in the caregiving process. When Grace turned away from her food, Iris saw this as an opportunity to ask if she was through eating. Iris interpreted Grace's cues and action as a cue that she was satisfied. Iris relied on the baby's information and participation to help Iris determine what was happening. By doing so, Grace's actions were understood. Because Grace's cues and actions were accurately read, the caregiver was able to provide more sensitive care. When there is a mutual relationship, care can be special and specific to the individual baby.

When you misread cues, you may misinterpret babies' behavior. Consider the following situation: Cole, a seven-and-a-half-month-old infant, would often cry during a diaper change when there appeared to be no distress. This confused her caregiver. Also, Cole was not very successful when she tried to sit up, creep, or crawl. The director and caregiver discussed Cole's behaviors. The director asked the caregiver what she thought was happening to Cole. The caregiver's response was, "Maybe she's a lazy baby." The director, replied, "I've never seen a lazy baby. All babies are motivated to move." Together they tried to understand Cole's behavior. After repeated evaluations by pediatricians and a lot of persistence on the part of the mother, Cole was diagnosed with a viral infection in her spine. Six months in a cast eliminated the problem. Had the adults not hung in there to reveal the source of the problem, Cole would not be walking today.

Try to understand the baby's point of view. What is it that will help the baby be satisfied? What is this baby's preference?

Cues are not always as dramatic as Cole's need for medical intervention. Be on the lookout for subtle cues that can be easy to overlook. When Frances walked by six-month-old Armand, the baby stopped playing, looked at Frances, and lightly cooed. Frances stopped and asked Armand, "Do you want me to be with you now?" When Frances sat beside him, Armand crawled into Frances's available lap.

Cole's dramatic experience is an example of how adults can be wrong about what they see going on with babies. In the case of Cole, it made the difference between whether she walked or did not. To avoid missed cues from babies, try to understand the baby's point of view. What is it that will help the baby be satisfied? What is this baby's preference? The only way to answer these questions is through repeated experiences with each baby and observing him or her as much as possible.

◆ Include Babies in Everyday Caregiving Routines

There are reasons why adults forget to invite babies to be part of their care. One reason might be because of the way you view time or tasks. Often, tasks are done in a hurry and care is not seen as part of curriculum. Asking infants to help takes more time initially. Another reason might have to do with what you believe about babies' capabilities. Sometimes it's easier to do *for* the baby instead of *with* the baby. Doing *for* the baby takes less time, but it can harm your understanding of a baby's individual needs. Avoiding these pitfalls allows caregiving routines, including eating, to be a wonderful time to fuel your relationship together.

When caregivers and babies enjoy each other's company, pleasurable moments occur.

It is important to allow babies to be part of their care process. Consider the following attitudes that are reminders to pay attention to babies' cues and provide responsive caregiving:

- ◆ Babies are dependent but not helpless.
- ◆ Babies are individuals with preferences.
- ◆ Caregivers need time to observe a baby before responding.
- ◆ Caregivers need to slow down and stay focused on the job at hand.
- ◆ Caregivers need to allow babies to participate in the relationship.
- ◆ Relationships in caregiving require full presence from the caregiver and baby.
- ◆ Babies are capable at their level of development.

The above behaviors form attitudes that support interactions that respect babies and allow them to cooperate in the caregiving process. By allowing babies to be active participants in their daily experiences, you give them opportunities to initiate and respond. The result is that babies become satisfied and content. In time, babies learn that they are an important part of the relationship with their caregivers.

Responding to baby's cues gives adults vital information for responsive caregiving. Trust the infant's ability to tell you what she needs. This can only be done if you slow down enough to observe. In order for the baby to communicate with you, she needs to be given time to express her needs. When you give babies that time, the babies' cues become valuable clues.

Key Point

By observing and interpreting the babies' cues, you can respond in sensitive ways that give babies the message that they are a valued participant in the caregiving process.

Solutions

◆ Respond to babies' cues and preferences to support their individual needs.

◆ Observe and interpret babies' cues as forms of communication.

◆ Caregiving times, such as eating, provide valuable opportunities for you and babies to exchange information that promotes responsive experiences.

Chapter 10

What Do Babies Need?

Issue

Primary caregivers (see Chapter 5—Primary Caregiving on pages 31–33) are key to the large amount of growth and development that occurs during the first year of life. Caregivers need to be knowledgeable about growth and development of babies in general and, specifically, of the babies in their care. They need to provide experiences that allow the babies to gain competence through the use of their bodies and their senses. When these opportunities are available for babies, they discover information and knowledge to help them understand the world around them.

Rationale

When you understand typical growth and development, you can use this information to guide your everyday actions by providing physical, cognitive, language, and social-emotional experiences for babies. Observing babies is one of the best ways to understand how they develop and to gain important information about each individual baby.

Goals

- ◆ To understand normal development and growth of babies
- ◆ To integrate sensory, motor, and language experiences in the daily life of babies
- ◆ To talk with babies about what is happening during care routines
- ◆ To understand that you are key to babies' early learning
- ◆ To acknowledge the importance of observation to understand babies' growth and development

In the first year of life, more learning and growth occurs than at any other time in life (Berk, 2005). Therefore, you need to be knowledgeable about the changing developmental needs of babies.

When you know what to expect because you know the guidelines for typical growth and development, you are able to understand the capabilities of babies at each stage of development. For example, Melanie, a new caregiver who had little experience working with mobile infants, saw Mary Jane cry as her mom walked out the door. Melanie looked confused about what to do for Mary Jane, so she continued to busy herself with morning chores as she told the baby, "You'll be okay." If Melanie knew about attachment, bonding, and separation at Mary Jane's stage of development, she might have responded differently and more appropriately by saying, "Mary Jane, mommy went to work. I know it upsets you when she leaves. It's okay to be sad; let me come near you to see if you want me to hold you now."

Because there is so much information available about the growth and development of infants, it may be hard to pick and choose what to read and what philosophy to follow. Choosing what to read, what to believe, and how to apply this knowledge can be an overwhelming task. On pages 188–189 of the Appendix is a chart showing some developmental characteristics of babies from one month old to 18 months old. Other suggestions include:

◆ Browse through or read professional child care magazines (for example, *Childhood Education, Child Care Exchange, Young Children*) to note which books they reference.
◆ Ask your child care director for articles he or she has found helpful on specific child care topics of your interest.
◆ Go online to Web sites of national child care organizations (for example, www.naeyc.org, www.rie.org, www.zerotothree.org) that endorse best practice for children.

Knowing what is typical growth and development for infants is a wonderful tool to help you understand what is happening with a baby and also why the baby is acting or behaving in a particular way.

Knowing what is typical growth and development for infants is a wonderful tool to help you understand what is happening with a baby and also why the baby is acting or behaving in a particular way. One developmental theory says in the first one and a half years of life, the infant derives pleasure and primarily learns through his or her mouth. Another theory states that the socio-emotional well-being of the infant depends on his or her ability to accomplish a trusting and mutual relationship with others. Still another theory talks about the infant in terms of his or her brain and motor development and describes the baby's abilities through movement and coordination. Each theory has contributed to what is known about babies. However, as caregivers, the issue is how you use what you know in your everyday practice with babies.

This baby is using his senses to stay fully involved in his play.

Magda Gerber, an infant specialist who worked most of her professional life with parents and their children in parent-infant classes, suggested watching and observing babies to learn about what infants can do and are ready to do. Gerber advocated the "readiness" model, or allowing infants to develop at their own rate. She loved to say, "The best book is what we learn from watching the babies, so observe more, do less."

◆ Sensory Experiences

In the first year of life, babies learn with their whole bodies through their senses of smell, taste, sight, sound, and touch. All of their senses are very alert. This lets babies absorb and take in what they experience in the moment, the here and now. As a caregiver, you need to provide sensory experiences for infants to help them develop. These experiences can happen any time throughout the day, and especially during caregiving times, by using simple techniques that include language, touch, sight, sound, and smell.

Here are a few examples of how to provide sensory experiences for babies:
- ◆ Make a point to let the baby hear the sound of water as you wash your hands after diapering the baby.
- ◆ Allow the baby to touch the wet washcloth or wipe before cleaning his or her bottom.
- ◆ Let the baby experience your touch for a longer period of time. Move away slowly.
- ◆ Because babies take more time to process information, slow down your actions to help the baby integrate and understand what is happening.
- ◆ Move close to the baby's face and let him or her see you when you are talking.
- ◆ Kneel down next to the infant on the floor so he or she can hear and see you.
- ◆ Allow the baby to splash a small amount of water in a basin.
- ◆ Let the baby feel the breeze outside.
- ◆ Ring a chime for the baby to hear.
- ◆ Hang a crystal in the room so the baby can see light reflected by the crystal.
- ◆ Sing a short rhyme or song to the baby.
- ◆ Hang a bird feeder to attract birds that the baby can see or hear.
- ◆ Let the baby see and touch a nontoxic plant.

Allowing babies to experience and learn from their bodies and from their senses enriches their daily experiences and provides important information for them to interact more fully in their environment. The following scenario describes a caregiver who appreciates how babies learn through their senses.

Carla picks up eight-month-old Juan from his crib and gives him a warm touch on his hand. "You had a wonderful rest," she says softly, close to his ear. Together they go to the feeding area where she runs water on his washcloth to clean his hands. When she notices that he is trying to grasp the water, she adjusts her body so Juan can feel the wetness on his hands. She says to him, "Yes, the water is wet and you seem to like feeling it." After drying Juan's hands with a soft cloth, she sits down with him and shows him the cereal and fruit for his lunch. Carla begins to wipe his hands with the wet washcloth as Juan grasps the cloth and sucks it in his mouth. "Does that feel good on your gums?" Carla asks. Carla waits for Juan to let go of the cloth before bringing his food closer. She brings the spoon closer to his mouth and waits for him to open his mouth to eat. Juan can smell the rice cereal and pears on the spoon that is near his nose and mouth. He opens his mouth wide and kicks his feet in anticipation of his first mouthful. Carla allows time for Juan to use his senses of smell, taste, touch, and sight to make connections to what is happening.

Your sensitivity to how babies learn about themselves and their surroundings is invaluable. Try the following when approaching a baby:

◆ Move slowly toward the baby.
◆ Touch him or her gently.
◆ Talk to the baby before picking him or her up to begin caring for him or her.
◆ Take time to include a few sensory experiences with the baby, such as allowing him or her to feel the water, washing hands, and giving soft touches.

Adding these few sensations is a wonderful way for the baby to learn and enrich his or her sensory experience. You can use your knowledge of the babies every day to help them experience the world around them.

◆ Movement

In the first years of life, babies goes through several progressive stages of movement, from lying on his or her back to sitting up, creeping/crawling, and standing upright and walking. Babies learn by moving. When babies move, it shows that their bodies and brains are working in coordination. Through movement, babies are able to practice and perfect their coordination as they repeat actions over and over and, eventually, attain certain skills. Reaching for objects as they explore develops their ability to choose as they decide which toy interests them or where they will move their bodies in space. By moving and exploring in their environment, babies gain knowledge and understanding. As they move and learn, they develop their cognitive abilities. Babies' ability to learn is related to their freedom to move, choose, and repeat their efforts. Through

Through movement, babies are able to practice and perfect their coordination as they repeat actions over and over and, eventually, attain certain skills.

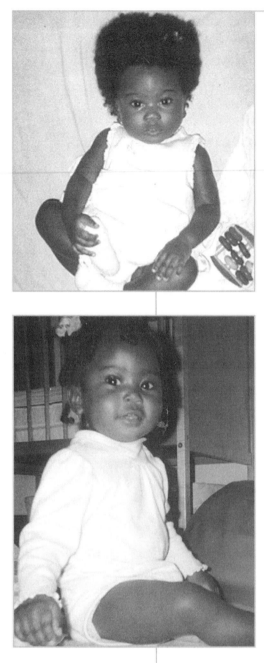

movement, babies are able to accomplish tasks that range from simple to more purposeful and complex tasks as they grow. Providing opportunities to babies for free movement and exploration is essential for their growth and development.

◆ Language

The first year also brings the development of language skills. At a few months old, most babies coo. At about three or four months, they make noises, often called raspberries, which are similar to puckering your lips to whistle. Babies learn to babble around six to seven months, saying a few things like "da-da" or "ma-ma." These are the baby's first syllables. Before the end of the first year, babies may say their first intentional word. For example, a baby may say, "cat" or "ball."

Because language is acquired in the context of everyday life, it is important to label objects aloud. To say, for example, "Here is a red ball," "This diaper is soft," or "Look at the blue bird." Talking with and telling babies what is happening is another way babies acquire language. Repeating short riddles, rhymes, or fingerplays to babies and playing a variety of music, such as songs with words or music that has a soft melody and no words, two or three times a day for 10–15 minutes offers a rich source of language development.

Babies acquire language by hearing it. They receive and absorb the language even though they cannot express the language. The best way to develop babies' language is to talk, read, and sing together. Describing what is happening during caregiving routines and dialoguing with the baby helps the baby to understand what is happening and provides sensitive interaction between you and the baby. Once babies understand what is being said to them, they can help in the caregiving processes. Make everyday occurrences a language-rich moment: "Come, I'm going to take you outside to play." "Look at the blue bird sitting in the tree." All these language cues will, eventually, have meaning for babies.

When babies grow and develop, they progress from lying on their backs to sitting and then moving about their environments.

◆ The Caregiver Is Key

You are very important to the physical, social, cognitive, language, and emotional growth of the babies in your care. Babies' earliest experiences with adults affect all future relationships. You are one of the adults who help form their world. You can help them develop by being respectful and nonjudgmental and supporting the baby's movement, language, and sensory experiences. Allowing babies enough time to think, feel, and experience what is happening to them promotes their ability to make physical and cognitive connections. These connections help to foster baby's development. When ten-month-old Bryon picks up the ball instead of the doll, he makes a conscious choice that demonstrates his preference. Providing opportunities for babies to have these experiences is respectful to babies' personal choices. Your role is to observe babies, allow them to explore their environment, assist them in their exploration, guide their explorations, and model interactions and explorations for them in ways that help develop and maintain responsive relationships they can rely on. When babies feel safe and secure in their relationship with adults, they are more comfortable stepping into and experiencing their world.

Key Point

Babies need rich sensory, language, and movement opportunities to understand themselves and how the world works. You are the key to introducing and integrating experiences for babies that include sensory, language, and movement opportunities. These experiences provide wonderful observational opportunities that allow you to learn about each baby's development.

Solutions

◆ Observe babies to gain important growth and development information.
◆ Allow babies free movement to learn about and experience themselves and objects in their environment.
◆ Include sensory-rich experiences in babies' daily experiences.
◆ Expose babies to several language opportunities throughout the day.
◆ The caregiving relationship provides a variety of learning opportunities in all developmental domains.

Expose babies to many language opportunities.

Chapter 11

The Baby Is the Curriculum

Issue

Accurate and timely care based on the individual needs of each baby and focused on the needs of each baby is the basis for any curriculum with infants. Room schedules, which many centers use, do not allow caregivers to respond to important cues given by babies.

Rationale

Babies need to be cared for by responsive adults who observe babies sensitively and interpret their needs. When this happens, babies develop a special bond with their caregivers because they feel understood. Because their needs are being met, this understanding builds trust and reinforces a positive care relationship (Honig, 2002; Kovach & Da Ros, 1998).

Goals

◆ To keep the caregiving process focused on the babies
◆ To read important cues that define babies' needs
◆ To maintain a relationship that reinforces individual care

If room schedules dictate when babies eat and sleep, even if they are not ready, then the individual needs of babies are unmet. If, however, the primary focus of the curriculum is the needs of the babies instead of a room schedule, then it is easy to remember what's important throughout the day—what babies need.

What does it take for each baby to get timely care? First, as an infant caregiver, you need to believe and see that the baby is the primary focus of each day. You have to believe and act in ways that support each baby's own sense of what he or she needs. This requires focus, knowledge of each baby, and keen observation.

Reading and interpreting the baby's cues keeps the focus individualized. While this can be challenging, it is what babies need to thrive and survive physically and emotionally. Consider the following interaction by Latisha, an observant caregiver: "Madeline, you look like you're getting tired. I saw you yawn and noticed how you rubbed your eyes. I am going to take you from the playroom and change your diaper before your nap." Latisha's observation was very accurate as seven-month-old Madeline soon fell asleep in the safety and comfort of her crib.

What does "the baby is the curriculum" mean? It means the baby comes first, and you should develop a special relationship and bond with that baby. You have to know the baby, and the baby has to know you, well enough for you to care for him or her. This type of relationship is built on an understanding of the baby and his or her needs and wants at a particular time and as they change over time. This takes an investment of time to relate to the baby and build a relationship together that is grounded in trust.

As an infant caregiver, you need to believe and see that the baby is the primary focus of each day.

The key elements to developing and continuing a trusting relationship with babies include the following:
- Observing what is happening with the whole child
- Providing a safe, calm, peaceful environment
- Giving each child one-on-one individualized attention
- Staying focused on the baby
- Creating consistent routines of care
- Providing choices and options that support babies' preferences
- Allowing the baby to help by participating in his or her care
- Talking with the baby about what is happening
- Providing responsive and respectful caregiving
- Waiting for the baby to respond and including his or her response in your next interaction with the baby

Responsive care requires a commitment on your part. Start today by choosing one thing to change and sticking to it as you take care of babies. Maybe you have already been thinking about babies in this way. If not, it may be time to start. Denise, an infant caregiver, decided to greet each baby by name every morning as part of how she recognized each individual baby. Over time, she began to notice how enthusiastically the babies anticipated their special greetings. Denise experienced firsthand the effect of how she treated babies. She could see that what she did made a difference. Kim, another infant caregiver, noticed how her babies liked the way she touched them. When she picked up a baby, she would be careful to move the baby respectfully from one place to another. Kim used the following method that you may want to try.

Kim's Method of Moving Babies Respectfully

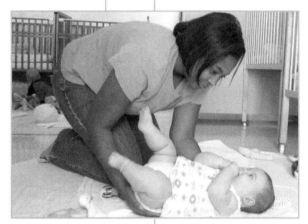

When picking up a baby, move the baby in respectful ways.

1. Go to the infant's level (in this example, the infant is on her back and you are on her right side).
2. Speak gently as a greeting and tell the baby you are going to pick him or her up.
3. Make eye contact with the baby.
4. Accommodate your body to the baby by moving closer to the baby. This may require bending.
5. Move slowly and wait for the infant's response.
6. Cross over the infant's body with your hand reaching the left shoulder of baby.
7. Place your left hand over left shoulder of baby who is on his or her back.
8. Place your right hand to support the baby's back.
9. Place your left hand behind baby's neck and head.
10. Move your right hand to the baby's mid-back.
11. Cradle the infant and lift him or her.

This gentle and careful handling helps develop a special regard for all babies in your care. By handling babies respectfully, you show them that they are valued, which helps their overall health and development to flourish.

Key Point

In center-based care, the baby is the curriculum. This is best done when you respond to cues babies give about what they need. Knowing each baby and responding to his or her individual needs builds trust and helps maintain an ongoing, respectful relationship between you and the baby.

Solutions

Curriculum is:
◆ Keeping each baby as the main focus in your caregiving
◆ Knowing how to read babies' cues about what they need
◆ Responding to each baby in an accurate and timely way

Chapter 12

The Caregiver As an Important Part of the Curriculum

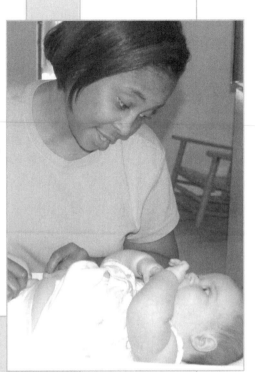

Issue

The caregiver is the most important "ingredient" in any curriculum, and in developing and providing a rich and meaningful care relationship with the baby. The babies' self-worth is dependent upon the attention, care, and respect he or she receives.

Rationale

As caregivers, when you believe that the baby *is* the curriculum, you will use your energy and time to get to know, understand, and be available to meet each baby's unique and individual needs.

Goals

◆ To promote relationships that are responsive to babies' cues and needs
◆ To understand that your attentive presence is vital to babies' well-being
◆ To allow babies to experience their environment, interact with the people around them, and initiate actions on their own during noncaring times
◆ To avoid encouraging dependency with babies
◆ To evaluate your motives and feelings about how you behave with babies

Even though the baby *is* the curriculum, there is a very important "ingredient" that needs to be included in the curriculum—*you*. Babies need you to help carry out the curriculum of the day. The majority of books about infants and what to do with them focus on experiences and activities that promote stimulation. Infant stimulation experts agree that infants need stimulation to grow and develop. The toy industry earns billions of dollars selling toys that buzz, bang, whistle, and clang; all say, "Baby, baby, pay attention to me!" These toys provide hours of entertainment for mesmerized babies, by stimulating and acting *on* babies. But, these toys deprive babies of valuable experiences that develop their own interests, sense of discovery, powers of concentration, and problem-solving skills, which will be useful to them throughout their lives.

Babies learn best and thrive through relationships with adults who care for them. Placing "busy toys" in front of babies is not the answer to developing a curriculum. The single most important factor in developing a curriculum for babies is *you*, the caregiver. You are the one who knows individual babies, and you have the opportunity to relate to babies in significant ways that tell each baby that he or she is special.

◆ Paying Attention to Babies

Bottle feeding can be a special moment for baby and caregiver alike.

Because you are the most important "ingredient" in developing a curriculum with babies, consider what to do with babies all day and how to do it. The best time to build a relationship is while the baby is awake and in need of care like feeding or diapering. Paying full attention to the baby who is with you gives that baby the message that he or she is worthy of this time and attention. Keri, a caregiver, is aware that her actions and reactions are key to the development of the babies in her care. For example, Keri loves feeding five-month-old Noah his bottle. Noah is eager and responsive in his sucking. Keri found through repeated feedings with Noah that he likes his milk slightly warmed. Noah sucks harder and tugs at his fingers when the temperature of his milk is just right. Keri makes a point of always having that just right temperature for Noah. Keri's sensitive observation and response to subtle cues from Noah tells him that he is important and special to her.

When you believe that the baby is the curriculum, you direct your energy to being present and available to babies. For example, you observe that Phoenix, a 12-month-old, is not hungry now. He is tired, but six-month-old Elise is very hungry. So you put Phoenix to sleep and feed Elise. Observing and evaluating each baby's needs allows you to know what to do at a particular time for each baby. Observation and many interactions will help you understand each baby's needs. The message you give babies during these care times is, "It's you and me together," whether you are putting them down to rest or changing their diaper.

◆ Babies Do Not Need to Be Entertained!

Sometimes caregivers fall into the trap of entertaining infants. Babies do not need to be entertained! Making them giggle, laugh, dance, and perform can be a nonproductive way for babies to experience their world. When you act upon babies in this way, it can rob them of their own initiative and creativity. It can foster a dependency. They begin to rely on you for entertainment and passively wait for you to entertain them again. For example, Cindy fostered a special relationship with 10-month-old Justin. In fact, she became so overly involved that Justin became overly dependent and began to rely on Cindy to be "ever present." One day Cindy tried to water plants, and Justin began to cry and fall apart. It took several minutes before Cindy could calm Justin down. This is an example of a caregiver who allowed a child to become overly dependent on her, disrupting the child's emotional stability. Justin's emotional dependence on Cindy caused a setback in Justin's social-emotional development. Finding an emotional balance in your relationships with babies requires you to consider whose need is being met and what is in the best interest of the baby's emotional well-being.

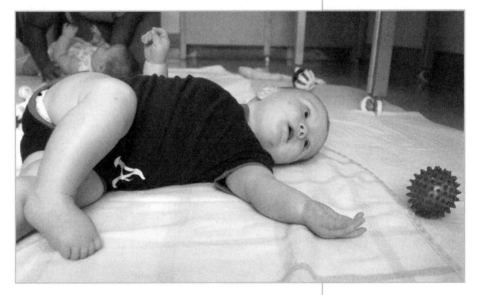

During many noncaregiving times, infants can entertain themselves. You can place babies on the floor where they can manipulate, discover, watch, coo, move, mouth, and suck in ways that only they would do at that particular time. Why teach babies to be emotionally dependent when they can initiate actions and choose how to interact in their environment!

Placing objects near the baby allows him to choose what he wants to grasp.

Key Point

When the curriculum focuses on the relationship between you and the baby, caregiving times become special one-on-one opportunities with babies. Babies get socially and emotionally "fueled" by these care routines, and do not need to be entertained at other times. Babies can be on the floor as they manipulate, move, watch, and discover their world. Finding balance in your relationship with babies in your care requires observation and assessment of needs—yours as well as the baby's.

Solutions

◆ Provide sensitive, caregiving opportunities that "fuel" baby socially and emotionally.

◆ Keenly observe babies' cues to support their preferences and give them individual care.

◆ Be present and available to babies during caregiving times.

◆ Separate your needs from those of babies to create a give-and-take, not dependent, relationship with the babies.

◆ Provide experiences for babies to play and explore on their own.

◆ Avoid entertaining babies or asking them to "perform."

Chapter 13

PR for Infants: Supporting Predictable Routines

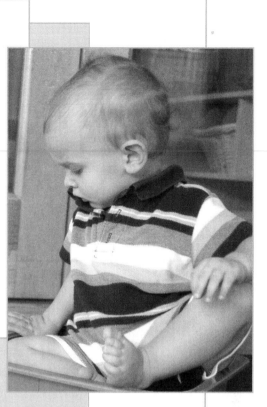

Issue

Interacting with babies during caregiving routines is the foundation for your relationship with babies. Routines help babies understand what is happening and trust that their needs will be met. When you carry out routines consistently, this stability lets babies know what to expect, and then they are better able to contribute in their care. Routines that are unpredictable compromise babies' sense of understanding and security.

Rationale

All babies need routines that are clear and consistent. Each time you diaper, feed, or put a baby to sleep for a nap, he or she learns to know and understand what you expect at those times. When you follow consistent daily routines, babies understand and trust what is happening. Consistent routines decrease anxiety and confusion for babies in group settings.

Goals

◆ To provide consistent care to babies based on routines
◆ To create routines based on a predictable sequence of events
◆ To provide routines based on babies' needs

Knowing the importance of routines is the first step to providing predictable routines. What exactly are routines, and why are routines so important in infant caregiving? Routines are patterns of care that, when done repeatedly, become expected. Examples of routines are diapering, feeding, and putting a baby to sleep for a nap. When routines are predictable, babies know what to expect and are able to trust their world and that their needs will be met. Routines assure a stable environment. When patterns are created and the caregiver is fully present when providing the care, the baby receives quality care. The baby is then assured that her needs are met in a timely fashion. Routines are developed around a sequence of events as opposed to time: this happens, then this happens, then this happens.

SCENARIO

Kayla is five months old and in group care. She wakes up from her nap, looks around the room, and begins to smile at Ms. Nicole, her caregiver. Nicole approaches Kayla's crib and greets her warmly. Ms. Nicole extends her arms to see if Kayla is ready to come out of her crib. Kayla kicks excitedly and smiles broadly. Ms. Nicole picks up Kayla and says, "I see you are ready to get up" as she goes to the diaper area with Kayla. After an unhurried diaper change, Ms. Nicole asks Kayla if she is ready to eat. Her excited response signals Ms. Nicole to take her over to the feeding area to prepare the meal. Kayla watches eagerly as Ms. Nicole fixes her bottle and cereal. Ms. Nicole puts Kayla on her lap and slowly feeds her cereal. When the cereal is gone, Ms. Nicole shows Kayla the empty bowl and presents the bottle to her. The infant grasps the bottle as she begins to lie back onto Ms. Nicole's lap and chest. Kayla sucks vigorously at her bottle, gazing contently at Ms. Nicole for short periods of time. Ms. Nicole responds by looking into Kayla's eyes as Kayla initiates eye contact.

This baby helps by grasping the bottle.

Each baby's individual body rhythm needs to be considered when providing routines of caregiving. The stability of the caregiver and continuity of care are important in creating and maintaining everyday routines of care for infants (Honig & Lally, 1988). So how do you provide consistent care for a baby who is in group care? The above scene shows Ms. Nicole's commitment to follow through the entire process of care with Kayla. Ms. Nicole is observing the baby and is tuned in to Kayla's needs. Her consistent, reliable, and sensitive interactions help to reassure Kayla. This reassurance comes from repeating the same behaviors over and over until they become patterns that the baby begins to rely on and trust (Elliot, 2003). This helps babies learn to expect their needs will be met (Honig & Lally, 1988).

The more you use routines to meet the needs of a baby, the more accurate your communication and care are for the baby. However, when caring for one infant in a group setting, there is a dilemma for the caregiver. Sometimes another baby wants something while the caregiver is taking care of a baby. One helpful way to solve this dilemma is to use your voice to acknowledge and tell the baby that she has been heard. "I hear you Anna Marie, and I will be with you when I am through with Tabia." This helps the baby learn to wait and understand that you will be coming soon.

The more you use routines to meet the needs of a baby, the more accurate your communication and care are for the baby.

Consider this situation. Michelle, an infant caregiver, has been asked to do a feeding. She places all four babies ranging from five to 12 months of age in a group-feeding table. Michelle gets four bowls of food and four spoons. She sits in her chair directly across from the infants and automatically begins feeding the infants from left to right. This requires picking up each spoon for each baby very quickly to appease the hungry and increasingly demanding babies. After a few minutes, Michelle is beginning to look frazzled. She is not able to keep up the pace of feeding all four hungry babies. Her frustration and impatience mounts to coincide with the rising distress of the babies. Have you been there? If you have, you know how it feels to try to feed several babies at one time. The problem is the routine has been created to save time rather than be what the babies need. Trying to feed several babies at once does little to satisfy the caregiver or baby. In group care, it is possible to feed many babies at once, but it is not acceptable practice. For very young babies, individual routines should be based on the child's need for food or care. Routines that are not chaotic allow the caregiver to maintain her emotional balance like in the previous example where Ms. Nicole fed Kayla.

These are important issues to consider when developing routines with infants in group care. You need to ask what works with each individual baby. It's also important to know what you believe about how babies need to be cared for because your beliefs are what you act on.

Let's look back at Michelle, the caregiver, as she tries to feed those four babies. Look at the situation from the babies' point of view. How must those babies feel? Hungry? Rushed? Maybe confused and certainly over-stimulated. What messages are the babies receiving from this routine? One message is to hurry and eat. There is not enough time for you, and it is a chore that has to get done. Another message is that you are not worthy of the time it takes for me to be present just for you.

When routines are rushed, babies' needs are compromised. When this happens, it is hard for babies to understand what their bodies are trying to say. If babies do not understand their own bodies, how can they begin to understand how to relate in their world? If that is their experience, they soon learn not to trust what their own bodies are telling them. Babies learn to trust in themselves from the adults who care for them. When babies know what to expect from their caregiving routines, they learn to rely, understand, and trust in themselves from the routines you create with them.

◆ How to Carry Out Routines

- ◆ Know the babies in your care.
- ◆ Observe each baby to determine needs and preferences.
- ◆ Be flexible, consistent, and clear.
- ◆ Expect babies to explore the environment using trial and error.
- ◆ Adjust routines as needed.
- ◆ Include the baby in his or her care.
- ◆ Commit to completing the cycle of care for each baby.
- ◆ Tune out distractions.
- ◆ Be fully "there" for that baby. Tune out distractions to be fully present just for that baby.
- ◆ Move slowly.
- ◆ Wait for babies' cues.
- ◆ Include a baby's cues before initiating your next response.
- ◆ Avoid interruptions during caregiving.
- ◆ Use normal language with the baby.
- ◆ Monitor your own behavior during routines.
- ◆ Keep a record of each baby's needs.
- ◆ Share with coworkers the routines that work for the baby.

The important issue in any routine is to provide individual care for babies in ways that each baby learns to rely and count on.

The important issue in any routine is to provide individual care for babies in ways that each baby learns to rely and count on. Routines need to be slow moving, clear, and consistent and provide a pleasurable experience for both the baby and you. Through routines, you provide a sequence of events to help the baby understand what is happening and what will happen. Routines help babies understand their value as human beings.

By streamlining each baby's care specifically to his or her needs, you say, "Yes I am here. I am listening. Your needs are important to me, and I am trying to be consistent so you can begin to rely on me." It takes the eyes and ears of a sensitive adult to conduct successful routines.

Key Point

Routines are important in the caregiving process. They need to be clear, predicable, and consistent based on babies' needs. When routines are predictable, caregivers show babies they can rely on and trust what is happening to them.

Solutions

◆ Create clear, consistent routines of care.
◆ Create routines that follow a predictable sequence of events.
◆ Create routines based on the individual needs of babies.
◆ Stay focused on the baby during caregiving routines.

Babies thrive when caregivers provide predictable routines.

Chapter 14

Valuing and Respecting Babies

Issue

Caregivers who relate to babies in positive social and emotional ways foster babies' feelings that they are respected.

Rationale

Routine care times are opportunities to respond to babies respectfully. This can be done by observing babies before acting and staying in the social-emotional moment with the baby.

Goals

◆ To provide routines that offer rich experiences to demonstrate respect for each baby
◆ To stay in the social-emotional moment with the baby

What comes to mind when you hear the word "respect"? One meaning, according to the dictionary, is "to hold someone in high regard." This means respecting who someone is and accepting their individuality. Respect also means showing others how much you care about them.

Many adults find it easier to show respect to adults than to children, but babies need to be respected just like adults. You may view babies as a "work in progress" or as needy and helpless. If you do, you probably act in ways that "do for baby."

Jared, a 13-month-old playing at a child-care center, crawls over to a low bench overlooking the outdoor playground. He climbs on the bench to get a better view of children playing outdoors. Rose, the caregiver, sees Jared on the bench and wordlessly removes him from the bench. Rose is fearful that he will fall and hurt himself. Her actions are a response to protect Jared. However, did Jared need protection at this time or was this action the need of the caregiver based on her own anxiety? Jared was surprised and disoriented when Rose moved him.

Does this tell Jared he is respected? Actions like the one described above give babies the message that their interests and abilities are not valuable. This can undermine their feelings of self-worth.

Some adults believe that babies are empty vessels that need to be taught and shown what to do by knowledgeable adults. They are eager to teach babies what to do rather than discover what babies have already figured out on their own. Consider the following two diaper-changing scenarios.

Allison is trying to get 13-month-old Tobias out for his morning walk before snack time occurs. She quickly goes to him to put on his shoes and socks before going outside. Tobias tries to grab his socks with his little hands to be helpful. Allison tells Tobias, "Let's hurry so we can go outdoors," as she takes his hands away from his socks and puts them on herself.

By hurrying to get Tobias outdoors was Allison respectful to Tobias? Why or why not? Was the caregiver responsive to Tobias's desire to help put on his socks? What message did she give Tobias? Sometimes caregivers forget to allow babies to help in their care. Let's rewrite this scenario to show respect for the baby.

Allison is trying to get Tobias outdoors for his morning walk before snack time. She realizes Tobias may be hungry before the walk is over so she offers Tobias half a banana. After finishing his banana, Tobias tries to be helpful by exploring how to put on his socks. Allison smiles at him and encourages him by saying, "I see you are trying very hard to help put on your socks." Allison then slides the sock over Tobias's heel and allows Tobias to pull on the rest of his sock. Allison repeats the process with his other foot, allowing Tobias to be successful. She gives the same time to Tobias when she puts on his shoes, letting him help put them on before going on their walk.

Being fully present emotionally during caregiving times gives babies rich social experiences.

Staying socially and emotionally in the moment allows Allison to observe that Tobias wants to help in his care. In the situation described in the above paragraph, Allison, the caregiver, was tuned in to and responsive to Tobias. How you approach and handle babies affects how babies' feel about themselves.

Respectful care guidelines include the following:
- Observe the baby for cues that help you understand the baby.
- Act with the baby to include the baby in his or her care.
- Be calm and gentle in your actions during caregiving times.
- Talk to the baby about what is happening.
- Be fully present emotionally during caregiving times.

These guidelines, when done during each care time, strengthen your relationship with the baby. These steps will automatically slow down your actions and allow more pleasurable social interactions between you and the baby.

Your respect shows you appreciate the baby. It sets the foundation for how the baby develops attitudes about himself or herself. *You* make the difference.

Key Point

Respectful caregiving positively affects the development of the baby's self-image and attitudes about himself or herself. Your commitment to give respectful care will result in the baby's growing confidence in his or her abilities and feelings of self-worth.

Solutions

◆ Observe the baby for cues that help you understand what the baby needs.
◆ Stay emotionally involved in the caregiving process.
◆ Acknowledge and include the baby in the care process.
◆ Relate with the baby peacefully and calmly.
◆ Talk to the baby about what is happening.

Chapter 15

Communicating With Babies

Issue

Your attitudes influence if, when, and how you communicate with babies. You may be unaware of the value of talking to babies directly. Maybe it has not occurred to you to use language to include the babies in communication. When you ignore babies, you tell them they are not valued. When you do not talk to babies, they are unlikely to understand what is happening with them.

Rationale

Talking *about* babies instead of *to* babies discounts them as individuals. Babies need to be part of the communication process. When you communicate with babies, it validates their self-worth. They will also have a better chance to understand what is occurring. Language provides a model for babies about how to communicate, and it serves as a vehicle to convey thoughts and feelings.

Goals

- ◆ To acknowledge each baby by name
- ◆ To talk directly to each baby about what is happening
- ◆ To talk to babies before touching them
- ◆ To refrain from talking about babies to others in the baby's presence

How many times have you watched this scene unfold? As you approach two women and a baby, you overhear one woman say, "What a precious baby! Isn't she cute! How old is she now? Does she sit up yet? Oh! Look at those bright blue eyes." The woman takes the baby's hands in hers and in a high-pitched voice exclaims, "Aren't you the cute one." She then talks with the mother about her baby.

You may have witnessed this scene countless times. Most adults talk to other adults about the baby in front of the baby. The problem with this is that even though the baby is the focus of the conversation, he or she is being described as if she is not there. Although it's probably not deliberate on the part of the adult, by not talking directly to the baby, the baby is disqualified on a personal level. Repeated encounters like this tell the baby she is insignificant. Acknowledging and speaking directly to the baby by name tells the baby he or she is respected as an individual. Magda Gerber used to tell the story of how her mentor Emmi Pikler first impressed her. When Dr. Pikler came to Magda's home to visit her sick child, Dr. Pikler talked to Magda's daughter using her name and getting information she needed directly from the child. This amazed Magda as it never occurred to her that her young daughter could give the doctor that information (Gerber, 1978; Gerber & Johnson, 1998). For many adults, it might not occur to them to talk directly to a child, let alone a baby.

It can be difficult to get into the habit of talking with babies. There is a vast difference between how babies communicate and how adults communicate. Babies use gestures and babble, which requires close observation. Also, most adults are better talkers than listeners. They are better at giving information than receiving it. Some adults think that babies do not have the ability to learn to comprehend. If you believe that, it's easy to understand why you do not address or talk to babies directly. These differences get in the way of responsive communication between adults and babies.

Repeated social encounters that are rich and spontaneous are what fosters the relationships between babies and caregivers. Relationships are the most important ingredient that fuels the baby and assures the baby's optimum health in his first year of life.

When babies trust their caregivers, their interactions are spontaneous.

What you believe and think about babies influences how you act. When you evaluate what you think about babies, you may decide it is worthwhile to talk with them. There are approaches to communicate with babies that convey a personal, respectful, and responsive message to them.

Talking to a baby requires you to

◆ Acknowledge the baby by name.

◆ Wait for the baby's response.

◆ Include your observation of the baby's response in your next message.

◆ Say what you see or think you see and include those responses.

The above suggestions allow you to experience an enriched dialogue with a baby. Sharing information provides more accurate and tuned-in communication where preferences and choices maintain a sense of who babies are as people.

SCENARIO

Sharon is feeding 14-month-old Allison peas and potatoes for lunch. Allison turns her head away from the spoon of peas after her first taste. Sharon, her caregiver, says, Allison you don't like the way these peas taste? You turned your head. Does that mean you don't want anymore?" Allison continues to turn away from the peas. "Okay, let's try some potatoes for now." This form of communication shows that the caregiver and the baby both are in tune to each other's behavior and watch each other's responses to continue more accurate communication together. This way of being together tells the baby her responses are acknowledged and included. Sharon may think peas are good for Allison but does not force Allison to eat them. By talking directly to Allison about what is happening, Allison is heard and respected for her preferences.

Eating peas is less important than the acknowledgement and acceptance of Allison's behavior about her preferences. As behaviors are repeated, Allison and Sharon learn and know more about each other, which develops trust and reliability in a mutually satisfying relationship.

Telling the baby what you are doing together during caregiving times is another important communication issue. Describing your actions with words helps the baby to understand and anticipate your next move. Telling the baby what you are doing together during caregiving times is another important way to communicate. Maria, the caregiver, began to put on 14-month-old Isabella's sweater to go out doors. Maria showed Isabella the sleeve of the sweater saying, "I'm going to put your right hand in the sweater." Maria then touched Isabella's right hand saying, "I'll start here." Isabella was prepared for Maria's signal and attempted to push her right arm through the sleeve of the sweater. Maria's words and actions signaled Isabella about what was going to happen, enabling Isabella to understand and cooperate with Maria. Knowing what comes next can reduce anxiety. Telling babies what will happen, showing them the steps along the way, and touching them to give them clues about what is happening is a powerful and wonderful way to give the baby a chance to understand your actions and intentions. These behaviors offer a rich dialogue between you and the baby that is a nice way for the baby to stay involved with you.

A few behaviors that help you give baby clear messages include the following:
- ◆ Calling each baby by his or her name
- ◆ Speaking directly to the baby
- ◆ Showing the baby the object or item you are focusing on
- ◆ Gently touching the body part you want to address
- ◆ Waiting to see if the baby will help
- ◆ Bending down to the baby's level
- ◆ Thanking the baby for his or her cooperation when it occurs

Maria's gentle touch signaled Isabella to participate. Touching gently is a wonderful way to show a tender response while communicating with babies. Touch can give the baby a warning that something is about to happen. A caregiver who gently touches a baby before picking her up by placing her hand on the baby's shoulder gives that baby a beautiful message of respect and appreciation.

There are so many small ways that you can communicate a message of worth to each baby. All you need to do is to stop, appreciate, and believe that your acknowledgment makes a difference. Trying these behaviors provides a valuable form of communication and a time to enjoy each others' company.

Key Point

Each baby needs to be acknowledged personally by name and given the opportunity to communicate. This ensures that babies understand what is happening. It also acknowledges their behavior and personal preferences as important.

Solutions

- ◆ Acknowledge each baby by name.
- ◆ Let babies know you believe they can contribute to an interaction or a relationship.
- ◆ Demonstrate and model to other adults how important it is to acknowledge and include babies in conversations.
- ◆ Think about babies' likes and dislikes when you communicate with them.
- ◆ Use gentle touch to signal and/or ask for participation.

Chapter 16

Babies Communicate By Crying

Issue

Babies cry for a variety of reasons. When they cry it is a signal that they need something. When babies cry, you may feel anxious or helpless and want to respond quickly to "hush the cry." You can identify why a baby is crying by taking time to understand and observing what is happening with the baby.

Rationale

As a caregiver, you need to identify why a baby is crying and to distinguish the different cries of each baby. This means taking the time to observe why the baby is crying and letting the baby know that you are trying to help.

Goals

◆ To observe to understand why the baby is crying
◆ To acknowledge that you hear the baby crying and are trying to help
◆ To identify that your feelings about crying may prompt you to act in a hurry to "hush the cry"
◆ To develop a checklist or record that helps you understand babies' patterns and needs

Crying is the way babies communicate what is going on with them. Because adults may have a hard time listening to a crying baby, they often pick up the baby to meet the baby's need quickly and to stop the crying. How do you respond when you hear a baby cry? How does it make you feel? A crying baby can make you feel uptight, helpless, frustrated, and maybe a little irritated or angry. One of the hardest tasks when caring for babies is to interpret what their cries mean while trying to maintain a sense of inner calm.

It is common to feel a little anxious when you hear a crying baby. While the actions you take to soothe the baby quickly may fill your need, it may not be what the baby is trying to tell you by crying. When you act too quickly, you may miss opportunities to try to understand what the baby needs. It can be hard to calm those strong emotions that produce anxiety, frustration, and sometimes even anger when you hear a baby cry.

Melissa, a caregiver in the infant room, stopped her supervisor one morning and said, "Can you help me? We have to do something about Quinn. He cries so much for no reason. I don't know how to help him. I've tried everything and nothing seems to work." Obviously, Melissa was frustrated about six-month-old Quinn. The supervisor helped Melissa identify the frustration she was feeling about Quinn. It is crucial to support and encourage caregivers to talk about what is going and how they are feeling. The supervisor gave Melissa permission to have her feelings without judging her. She also arranged for another person to care for Quinn temporarily to give Melissa a break. The supervisor provided some possible reasons why Quinn was crying and offered suggestions. One suggestion was to take Quinn outside to be closer to nature. Maybe this would help to soothe him. Another idea was to place Quinn beside another baby who was at the same developmental stage. Expanding Quinn's world in these ways had a positive effect and helped to reduce Quinn's crying. As Quinn developed his motor skills, he cried less. Melissa noticed that Quinn stayed interested in his new explorations. As time went on, Melissa and Quinn began to develop a closer and more relaxed relationship. Melissa learned that sometimes babies, like Quinn, get stuck in a particular stage, become unhappy, and are unpleasant to be around. Once Melissa was able to realize that she was not the cause of the problem and that this was a temporary stage, she was able to feel more positive about Quinn, and she was able to change her attitude about him.

SCENARIO

As babies develop, their cues become easier to distinguish. Their different cries tell us what specific need they are trying to communicate. "Oh, that's Regan's hungry cry," or "I can tell Jameel is really tired by his cry" are examples of adults "knowing" and understanding a baby's specific cry. When caregivers spend time with babies, they are able to interpret the meaning behind the baby's cry and respond accurately.

When babies cry, it is useful to go through a mental checklist. Is she wet? When did she last eat? Is she overtired? Did something frighten her? Is she uncomfortable, possibly too hot or too cold? Remember, crying is a primitive urge and may even be a way to release energy. Understanding the reasons for babies' cries is a trial-and-error process. Until you get to know the baby, keeping a daily record of care will help you understand the baby's patterns and needs.

◆ Identify Your Feelings

Understanding the reasons for babies' cries is a trial-and-error process.

When a baby cries, you may feel helpless. If the baby continues to cry, you may become anxious. One caregiver told the story of how upset she became when she heard another baby continue to cry as she was caring for another baby. She said she felt trapped and embarrassed when her coworker turned around to look at her as if to say, "Do something about the crying baby." It is easy for caregivers to consider a baby's cry as a reflection of whether they are good caregivers. Often peers react with disapproval when a baby cries, reinforcing your self-judgment. Whatever the reason, you may react to the pressure that something must be done to stop the crying baby. However, it is not always possible to know how to soothe a baby and you may feel uneasy about how others will judge your abilities. This is especially true in group care situations at early arrival and late departure times. When there are more adults around, there may be added pressure to hush the baby. Adults often equate good care with happy babies, not babies who are crying. This spoken and unspoken expectation adds pressure on caregivers to try to maintain a room full of babies who are not crying. Even though you know that babies cry for a variety of reasons, you may still get nervous when they do.

A mother who is bringing her baby into the infant room hears Tahisha, a four-month-old baby in her crib, who is crying. Beverly, the caregiver, says to Tahisha, "You'll be next after I finish with Dante." After the mother settled her baby, she noted the baby was still crying. She went over to the feeding area to ask Beverly and the other caregiver, "Aren't one of you going to find out what she wants?" Beverly looked up and said, "I know it's hard to hear Tahisha's cry. A few minutes ago she was sleeping peacefully. Dante needs to finish eating. When we pick up a baby to care for that baby, we finish with that baby before picking up another baby. We use our voice to let the baby know we hear her cry and will be there soon." Later, when the mother returned, Beverly had some free time to check in with the mother about her feelings. Beverly was able to explain to the mother the importance of each baby getting care to satisfaction and that when another baby cries, one of the caregivers acknowledges the baby's cries by talking to the baby to let the baby know that her cries are heard and that her needs will be met soon.

When you hear a baby cry, remember to follow three steps: observe the baby, acknowledge the baby's cries and needs, and relax, moving toward the baby as soon as possible.

◆ Observe the Baby

How should you respond when a baby cries? First, observe the baby before acting. This requires time to look and connect with the baby. Take a deep breath and remind yourself that observing and trying to figure out why the baby is crying is an important way to identify the type of care you need to give the baby. Giving care that is tuned in to the needs of the baby leads to a better chance that the baby's needs will be met. In her book, *Your Self-Confident Baby* (Gerber & Johnson, 1998), Magda Gerber suggests "observe more, do less." However, observation takes time, and sometimes babies will cry for a longer period of time as the caregiver tries to figure out how to help them. Don't give up. Soothe and calm the baby by saying in a very soft voice, "I hear you. I don't know why you are crying. Let me try to help you figure out what you want." The baby may respond to your calm and soothing voice. Using your voice to signal the baby is a better way to acknowledge what the baby is feeling than putting a pacifier in his or her mouth.

◆ Acknowledge the Baby's Cries and Needs

When you are working with a group of infants and one baby cries, you may not be able to go to that baby immediately because you are with another baby. It is okay to acknowledge the crying baby by saying, "I hear you crying, Samantha. When I finish with Alex, I will come to you." Using voice control allows the baby to recognize that you heard her. This personal response between you and the baby often is enough to help the baby learn to trust you will be coming. This can reduce the amount and length of the baby's cry. Over time this acknowledgement may help babies to learn to wait. It's important to go to the baby as soon as you finish what you are doing. This helps babies to develop trust that they will get what they need. Recognizing your emotions and responding to babies' emotional needs is the "glue" that binds babies and caregivers in the caregiving process. A little emotional "refueling" given at the right time can offset many a cry and diminish the amount of crying time for the baby.

◆ Relax

Try to relax when caring for babies, even if the baby begins to cry. Understanding and believing that crying is a response to a need and not a negative message may help you relax. However, it is still important to **respond to the baby's cry as soon as you are able** and to try to figure out why the baby is crying. Babies communicate their thoughts and feelings through cries. For instance, some babies cry when they are exposed to too much stimulation. In child care settings, babies may cry more when there is too much noise or activity. Babies also cry when they are over-tired, when they first wake up from napping, when they are put down for nap, or when you change their position from one place to another. It is common for babies to cry when you leave abruptly without giving the baby enough time to process what is happening. Some babies cry when you rush or hurry them. In short, babies often cry during transitions regardless of how small they seem to you.

Key Point

Babies cry as a form of communication and for many reasons. Finding the accurate response to a baby's cry will end the baby's distress and your feelings of tension as well. Observing the baby as a first step allows you to gain a more accurate assessment and respond appropriately to the baby's need. Acknowledging that the baby is heard is one way to calm the baby as you try to find the appropriate response.

Solutions

- ◆ Observe the baby before trying to "hush the baby's cry."
- ◆ Let the baby know that he or she has been heard.
- ◆ Try to learn the different cries of each baby.
- ◆ Keep a record of the baby's pattern of need.
- ◆ Identify and understand your feelings when you hear a crying baby.
- ◆ Identify why the baby is crying.

Chapter 17

How Infants Interact with Each Other

Issue

Babies like to communicate, interact, and explore each other when they are together. You may be afraid that babies will hurt each other, so you prevent babies from interacting together.

Rationale

Babies learn about human relationships when they are able to interact with each other. Your role as the caregiver is to allow these important interactions to occur within safe limits.

Goals

◆ To identify attitudes, fears, and beliefs that prevents you from placing babies near each other
◆ To increase your comfort level about babies interacting with other babies
◆ To allow babies in the same or compatible developmental stages to be near each other
◆ To watch babies interact while monitoring their interactions for safety
◆ To model gentleness to both babies when struggles occur between babies

These babies, who are at the same developmental level, are able to safely watch each other, touch each other, and explore their environment together.

Placing babies who are at the same developmental level together (for example, crawling babies with crawling babies) gives them a chance to learn and explore who the "other" is. By watching, touching, and being near one another, babies experience a broader social world. As you take time to observe how babies interact with one another, you can begin to appreciate how valuable these experiences are for babies. Providing a safe environment for babies to be together during exploration and play times allows you to enjoy each other. Some caregivers try to keep babies separated from one another because they are afraid that infants may hurt each other, or because they may not think that babies' interactions are useful or important. These attitudes or beliefs influence whether you allow babies to be together or separate them from each other. When infants move around freely, your anxiety may stem from fear that something terrible might happen to one of the babies.

SCENARIO #1

A consultant who was visiting an infant room noticed that most babies were in swings, cribs, playpens, and bouncy chairs. She watched a baby who was on the floor slowly approach a baby who was nearby. Both babies were at the same stage of development. The caregiver, who was feeding a baby, stopped feeding the baby, drew in a deep breath, ran over, and scooped up the creeping baby. She verbally scolded the baby in her arms, who started crying, and then placed this crying baby in her crib.

Obviously, the caregiver thought the mobile infant was going to hurt the other baby. We will never know what might have happened between the two babies because the caregiver acted so quickly to remove the one baby from the other. In doing so, the babies were denied an opportunity to be together and interact. The message to the mobile baby was that she did something wrong. Her crib became a mild form of punishment. What a different message the mobile infant could have received from the caregiver if her actions were less intense! Maybe all she needed to do with the mobile baby was observe and move closer to see if she would be needed for the safety of the babies. Grouping children at the same level of functioning, based on stage rather than age, can offset the problem and allow babies to be together with each other. This would also help the caregiver be less anxious and stay involved with feeding the baby.

Natasha, a fairly new caregiver, mentioned her discomfort when babies get too close to each other. Her discomfort stemmed from the belief that babies are not able to judge their own capacities. She felt the babies would hurt one another if placed close to each other. Natasha's director asked her if it would make a difference if she put two babies together that were at the same level in their development. For example, two babies lying on their backs but not rolling over yet. Natasha said she wasn't sure. Natasha asked the director be available and watch nearby to see what the babies would do. Natasha was surprised when the babies looked, babbled, and reached toward each other. "It seems like they are really happy and enjoying being together," Natasha stated. During the length of time Natasha stayed, she observed the babies to be safe. She repeated her observations with older babies who could roll over and with babies who could sit up. She found when babies at the same stage of development were together, they appeared to enjoy one another, and safety was less an issue. Natasha became comfortable and less anxious with babies being together and provided times for that to happen in small, compatible-stage groups.

When you think about it, isn't it better for babies to have an opportunity to watch each other, be near one another, and be able to touch another person as long as it is safe? Being able to touch another human gives the baby a chance to expand his or her social world.

Babies enjoy being together.

Here are some guidelines to help you be more comfortable with babies being together:

◆ Place babies at the same level of development near each other.

◆ Place babies near each other based on their ability to move and function in similar ways (for example, babies who are sitting up with other babies who are sitting up, and so on).

◆ Keep the group size small—two or three babies at one time.

◆ Make sure babies' physical needs have been met (eating, sleeping) before placing them near each other.

◆ Sit nearby to watch how the babies interact.

◆ Get involved for safety reasons only, unless the baby signals that he or she wants you to be involved, for example, by crawling in your lap. Let the baby be the initiator.

◆ When babies begin to show signs of conflict or if you think one is about to be hurt, model gentleness by showing gentleness to both infants. Gently touch the side of each baby's face saying, "Be gentle." This allows both babies to hear and feel gentleness on their body. You teach gentleness by being gentle.

◆ Acknowledge the baby who signals that he wants to hear from you (for example, by looking your way) by reporting what you see happening. "Luke, I saw you crawl up the slide; you must be pleased with yourself."

◆ Relax, observe, and enjoy babies during their explorations.

By providing time for infants to be close, you can learn to appreciate the budding social relationships that emerge. You can also learn from babies, including how to relax and appreciate each other in the present moment. When you allow yourself time to watch babies, you will see and experience how much they communicate with each other. When you move past your fears and bias and observe babies interacting and communicating, you will see that babies can learn from each other. Enjoy these pleasurable moments by quietly watching and monitoring the babies.

Key Point

Letting babies who are in compatible developmental stages be together and interact creates an opportunity for them to be with each other safely. There are valuable learning opportunities when babies interact.

Solutions

Caregivers maintain safety and model gentleness.

◆ Take time to observe infants interacting with each other.
◆ Value babies as social beings.
◆ Place babies who are in compatible developmental stages near each other.
◆ When conflict arises, teach gentleness by being gentle.

Chapter 18

Quality Time With Infants

Issue

Babies need quality time with adults who are emotionally present. Paying full attention to babies and putting your emotions into your actions creates quality time. Quality time allows the emotional relationship between you and babies to flourish.

Rationale

All babies need to feel valued. When you are fully present with a baby, even for short periods of time, the baby feels that he or she is important because someone is paying attention to him or her. Caregiving times are perfect opportunities to share quality time with babies in your care. Even a little quality time lets a baby know he or she is valued.

Goals

◆ To be emotionally available during caregiving times
◆ To enjoy "want-nothing" time with babies
◆ To understand that quality time is based on the emotional richness of an experience, not the length of time

Quality time has to do with the type of relationship and kind of presence you give to the baby. In reality, a little quality time goes a long way to develop emotional relationships with babies.

Americans like the idea of *more*—more cars, bigger houses, and lots of clothes—and value the concept that more is better and a lot is best. But, caregivers may not be as generous about giving their time when it comes to being emotionally present and developing relationships with babies. Caregivers are masters at multitasking while caring for babies. When this happens, you can miss opportunities to give babies quality time. However, less time can work if it is quality time because the value of time is its quality not its quantity. This is a time when less is more. Giving a baby your full attention for a short period of time satisfies and "fuels" the baby socially and emotionally. These rich, sensitive experiences can reduce the length of time that babies need to interact with caregivers about their needs because they were satisfied when their needs were met. Building quality relationships with babies isn't about length of time. It requires presence, attention, and being "fully there" (Gerber, 1979). It means giving a baby your "full attention" for a short period of time.

SCENARIO

Merlene, a caregiver of a five-month-old, said, "I plan for time to be near Amanda talking to her as she plays on the floor. I try to do this a few times a week for a few minutes to let Amanda be with me. I really don't want anything from her, and Amanda doesn't usually need something. So we just enjoy each other's presence. I think this tells her that she is important enough for me to give her my time. After all, time is the one thing you can give someone to let them know they are special."

Being "tuned in" means paying attention to the baby, whether diapering, feeding, or just being with the baby.

When adults relate to babies, they need to experience a sense of "time in." Time in" means paying attention to the baby whether diapering, feeding, or just being with the baby. It is giving, taking, sharing, and enjoying in the moment, the here and now, with the baby. These tuned-in times allow rich emotional interactions that deepen relationships between you and the babies in your care. It can be an invigorating and "refueling" time for both you and the baby. It is important for you to understand that this type of time makes a difference in the babies' development.

At a child development center, Lou Alice, a caregiver, was feeding Jennifer, a mobile infant at the weaning table. The lunch lasted about 20 minutes while the caregiver gave her full attention to the baby. When Lou Alice asked Jennifer, "Want more carrots?" or said, "Jennifer, these are carrots," Lou Alice was acknowledging the baby.

Asking Jennifer if she would like milk and waiting for her response showed Jennifer that she was respected as a person. Babies who are in group care need to be treated in this way. This simple, unrushed way allowed the baby to have a quality eating experience.

When this type of quality time occurs repeatedly, it develops and satisfies babies' need for social interaction. This frees you to have more time to accomplish what needs to be done because you have met the babies' needs during caregiving times.

Key Point

Quality time is based on being emotionally present with a baby. These times let the baby know he or she is acknowledged and valued.

Solutions

- Spend time each day being emotionally present with each baby in your care.
- Balance quality time with alone time for yourself.
- Do not multitask while with a baby.
- Meet babies' emotional needs during caregiving opportunities.

Chapter 19

Providing *Just Enough* Help to Babies

Issue

Caregivers often question how much or how little help to give babies. Through observation and trial-and-error experiences, you can learn how and when to be available to help babies. Helping babies means being to be able to respond physically and or emotionally to them.

Rationale

Developing a sensitivity to know *when* and *how* to be available with babies develops with experience over time. Providing *just enough* help for babies to succeed is an important skill to acquire.

Goals

◆ To find the balance between how much and how little to allow babies to work on their own challenges
◆ To allow the baby's behavior to guide your actions; his or her feedback will help you to know if your actions are helping or hindering him or her
◆ To assist babies in developing problem-solving skills
◆ To learn the long-range effects on babies of "rescuing" them
◆ To develop the art of knowing when and how to intervene in a given situation

Knowing how to intervene and when and how to be available to help babies requires repeated observation and judgment. Caregivers can sometimes fall into the trap of offering too much help before seeing if the baby can work it out. It can be hard to wait for the baby's response before acting, and to know when and how to be involved during babies' emotional and social situations.

Your beliefs and feelings about what babies are capable of influences how you respond to babies. In addition, if babies respond with a strong emotion, such as crying out or kicking their legs, you may find it difficult to deal with the situation. One reason you may find it uncomfortable to handle these situations is the baby's emotional responses may trigger feelings that impact your actions. When it comes to responding to babies' social and emotional struggles, caregivers generally fall into two categories. Some caregivers "freeze up" because they are unsure of what to do to help the baby. When caregivers feel anxious and confused about the baby's emotional responses, it can increase the caregiver's feelings of helplessness, which makes it even harder to decide how to act. The second category is caregivers who feel that the baby's emotional struggle is causing the baby to be uncomfortable. They may feel that there is not a workable solution to what is happening. In an effort to rescue the baby, the caregiver moves quickly to rid the baby of obstacles. This caregiver gives too much help too quickly in an effort to relieve the baby's dilemma. Consider the following scenario.

SCENARIO #1

Will, an 11-month-old mobile infant, climbs up on the slide structure with ease. When he is ready to get down, he hesitates and begins to whine softly. Ruth, the caregiver, immediately comes to Will's rescue by removing him from the slide, taking Will in her arms, and saying, "There, there, I've got you now."

◆ When to Support Babies' Own Efforts

Ruth appears to feel that Will is afraid and is not capable of getting off the structure, even with assistance. Therefore, she rescues him from what she views as an intolerable situation. This is an example of a caregiver's quick response, showing how adults can "jump in too soon" and give too much help. How might this situation been handled differently? Acknowledging his dilemma and moving in closer might have been a first response to see if he could figure out a way to get down from the slide. It is common for adults to be eager and available to solve problems for babies. This can rob a baby of a valuable opportunity to figure out ways he can solve his problem.

If Ruth felt that Will needed help, she could help guide him down the slide just enough for Will to get down on his own. Will's effort allows him to develop his skills. The more you allow children to try, the more they will try. Robbing young children of the possibility of "trying" has serious implications. The message given is, "You need me to solve this for you." Children will then learn to depend on others rather than themselves. This influences whether they will try to figure things out next time or wait for help. In one of Magda Gerber's lectures, she stated, "What we, as adults, do for babies, is what they learn to need." Helping babies to be more independent is a way to reinforce their confidence and competence.

On the other hand, sometimes adults do not offer assistance when babies need it. When this happens, the baby may become frustrated and overtired as he repeatedly tries to resolve the situation without adult help. When babies go beyond their endurance, it serves no purpose. Letting babies problem solve on their own when they need assistance, and allowing babies to fall apart serves no valuable purpose.

With babies, it is difficult to know when and how to be available. It may be hard to believe babies can be capable and resourceful in a variety of situations. It can be confusing to figure out what kind of help to offer in a timely way for the baby. The answer is simple: Let the baby be your guide. His or her reaction to your behavior will tell you if you are helping or hindering him or her.

Another issue is deciding how to intervene. In many child care facilities, caregivers do not place babies together because the underlying fear is that babies could hurt each other. This fear and the desire to protect babies prevent many adults from allowing babies to interact with one another.

SCENARIO #2

Kelly, a caregiver who was working in an infant room, was quietly folding laundry (a task that caregivers do frequently) and noticed nine-month-old baby Carey crawling toward a less mobile four-month-old baby lying on her back. As Carey got closer to the baby, Kelly became nervous. When Carey approached the other baby, Kelly ran over and scooped Carey into her arms and said, "Carey, no, no, you can't go over to that baby. She may get hurt by you." Kelly proceeded to put Carey in a bouncy seat. This well-meaning caregiver was trying to protect the baby from Carey, assuming the baby would be unsafe with Carey.

Keeping babies away from one another can be a full-time job in an infant room. What do you think Kelly could have done in this situation to have acted more respectful in her approach?

◆ Kelly could have moved closer to be available to protect the younger baby, if needed.

◆ Kelly could have placed babies together who were at the same compatible stage of development.

◆ Kelly could have provided a protected area for younger babies so older infants could not reach them.

Would this have offset Kelly's concerns? Allowing same-stage babies to be in close proximity to each other requires a certain mind set. The caregiver must value the infant's social development. If the caregiver does, he or she needs to trust that babies can be curious about each other without being in danger as long as proper adult precautions have been addressed. If Kelly needed to act, maybe she should have done it differently. If there was another caregiver in the room, she could have asked her to monitor the infants' play. If Kelly had to do something, she could have moved closer and safely guided the infant's behavior.

Caregivers need to promote positive social interactions while they safeguard babies. While this may not be easy, it is an important caregiving task.

Caregivers need to promote positive social interactions while they safeguard babies.

Developing strategies for infants to have options, choices, and discovery opportunities is challenging and takes thought and commitment. It means believing that what happens around physical, social, and or emotional situations with babies affects their learning process. How you handle these situations will make a difference in how babies view their own abilities and how they learn to interact with others.

Observing if, when, and how to be available to babies is an art.

Key Point

Figuring out *when* and *how* to be available to assist with infants and developing an understanding of how to provide *just enough* intervention takes time, patience, and observation.

Solutions

◆ Observe the baby's response to figure out if you are giving too much help or not enough help to babies. Repeated, timely interventions will make a difference in how babies are supported, which will affect how they learn to relate to others.

◆ Avoid "rescuing" babies too soon. Instead, guide them in their problem solving. Observing, interpreting, and responding to cues from babies will help to determine if and when help is needed. This develops the baby's problem-solving strategies and capabilities.

◆ Avoid analysis paralysis, which occurs when you are unsure about what to do to help babies. This lack of confidence causes indecision that prevents you from taking action (Gonzalez-Mena & Eyer, 2004).

◆ Be aware of what effect the baby's physical and or social-emotional struggles have on your feelings.

◆ Pay attention to your own feelings so that you don't "freeze up" or act too quickly in response to the baby's situations.

Chapter 20
Babies Learn By Struggling

Issue

It may make you uncomfortable to see babies struggle. Babies struggle socially and emotionally, for example, when two older infants hold onto the same toy and neither is willing to let go. Each tries to gain possession of the object and they become quite vocal in their struggle to gain control of the toy. As babies' emotions run high, you may feel uncomfortable. Because of this, you may try to prevent struggles or bring your own justice to a situation.

Rationale

Caregivers need to understand that struggles help babies to develop problem-solving skills and experience peer relations. It is best for caregivers to monitor and respond to babies' struggles when necessary to help babies develop positive social behaviors that promote learning.

Goals

- ◆ To identify how you feel when babies struggle and how that affects your behavior
- ◆ To allow babies to struggle within the limits of safety
- ◆ To avoid making judgments that promote your own concept of "justice"
- ◆ To stay focused on babies' struggle and not be attached to a certain outcome

Two mobile babies are on the floor in the play space. Soft music is playing against the natural background of chirping birds. The early morning sun is shining into the room creating a feeling of warmth. Your job is to make sure the children are safe while they play. As you sit nearby, you notice one of the babies crawling and creeping toward a baby who is babbling, tonguing, and sucking a teething ring. The baby appears totally involved in the object and does not see the approaching baby. The crawling baby sees the teething ring moving in the air, and she grasps the object and tries to pull it toward her. But it only goes so far and gets stuck. The baby looks away from the object and for the first time sees the arm of another baby holding the teething ring. Both want the object. They begin to push, pull, grunt, and scream in outrage. Thus begins the struggle.

As the caregiver in charge of the safety in the play area, what are you going to do? Most likely, you will act based on your beliefs about struggle, conflict, sharing, safety, and other related values you have learned in your life. Most people have a hard time with struggle. What you may miss is how struggling fits into the development of socialization (Da Ros & Kovach, 1998).

Basic personality traits also affect our response to struggle. Maybe you are the kind of person who likes to see that all goes well and want things to be put right. Then, what you decide to do will be based on your idea of what's fair and just. One caregiver mentioned that it was particularly hard to watch babies struggle because when she grew up, fighting and having disagreements was not allowed. She learned to avoid conflict and struggle to deal with problems. Watching babies struggle makes her uncomfortable. She sees monitoring babies while they are struggling as doing nothing.

Struggle is one way of putting forth an effort, and it usually it occurs during a conflict. A conflict is a situation with at least two opposing views. The struggle described above is that each baby wanted the same object and was trying to capture the object.

It can be hard to support the idea of allowing struggle. Most of the time, adults try to accomplish the opposite. However, it is impossible to avoid, eliminate, and prevent struggle and conflict from happening. Young babies usually struggle when physically stuck, such as when they get trapped between two pieces of furniture, or uncomfortable, such as when they are hungry, or when they grab an object that another baby is holding. There are many studies and research projects that focus on play and the outcomes of play, and much has been written about conflict and how to manage conflict (Bayer, Whaley, & May 1995; Da Ros & Kovach, 1998; DeVries & Zan, 1996). Piaget (1965/1932) considered conflict critical to development and necessary to children's learning. More recently DeVries and Zan (1996) asserted "conflict within an individual and conflict between individuals is essential in the development of the personality and the social and moral feelings that emerge from those situations" (p. 109). Some behavioral psychologists feel that providing the exact toys at the same time for all the infants would eliminate conflict over objects, but field observations showed no difference in how infants related to each other around struggle when several of the same toys were available to them. In other words, six rattles for six babies does not eliminate the struggle between babies. Kallo and Balog (2005) found that "even when children have enough toys to satisfy their interest, it sometimes happens during play (especially during the collection phase) that they take from the other" (p. 43). One possible reason is that babies like to grasp objects that are moving and active, such as those that other babies are holding.

Why does struggle have such a negative quality? For the baby, struggle is a natural occurrence. It is a way for babies to learn how things work. By observing the efforts of an infant during a struggle, you can see the ways individual babies relate to what is happening. You can watch how they approach and solve their dilemmas. Maybe these struggles help to form their personalities. Maybe struggling helps them to develop social relations and problem-solving skills.

In the mid 1980s, Magda Gerber spoke at a national conference about babies struggling. Her view was different from the popular view about struggle and how to avoid it. Magda felt that struggle was a natural part of life and that allowing the process to occur provided babies with valuable learning opportunities: "Infants learn what it is they can and cannot do, how to handle difficulties, and valuable lessons in problem solving." In Magda Gerber's view, working through struggles taught children how to handle different situations and that, in life, sometimes you win and sometimes you lose. She allowed babies to interact and solve their own dilemmas while monitoring them for safety so they would not harm each other.

If you watch babies struggle over an object, they are fully involved in what they are doing. They appear purposeful, intent, and interested. Maybe babies are less anxious around struggle than their caregivers.

Babies can be intentional when reaching for objects.

Caregivers usually have a hard time watching babies struggle without making a judgment or trying to fix the problem quickly. Many caregivers have a hard time refraining from stopping the struggle and often feel uncomfortable about what is happening. The babies, on the other hand, are totally involved in the pure act of struggle. Because babies move their bodies to learn, maybe their curiosity and interest in moving objects in another baby's hands adds another dimension. Maybe the object appears more alive and active and is quite an enticement to the baby.

If you can succeed in accepting struggle as a natural part of life, then you have to deal with your feelings about sharing. Why is it so important to teach sharing at such an early stage when babies cannot grasp such a complex concept? It is unrealistic to expect babies to understand the concept of sharing. Sharing is a social skill that adults model and underscore repeatedly for the young child. A four-year-old may be ready to listen about sharing, but developmentally, a baby cannot hear the same message. What is developmentally appropriate for older stages of development is not appropriate for babies.

When you begin to see that struggling is natural and logical, then the next challenge is what to do when you see struggling occur. When infants are in groups, struggle happens often unless you try to keep infants apart. Preventing babies from interacting and experiencing each other is not good for their social-emotional development.

When a struggle occurs between two babies, consider the following suggestions, using the ones that apply to the specific situation:

◆ Move nearby and watch the infants interact.
◆ Move slowly and talk slowly.
◆ Maintain safety to make sure babies do not harm each other.
◆ Be patient and don't overreact to the situation.
◆ Stay calm, because anxiety promotes anxiety.
◆ When one baby appears uncomfortable with what is happening, quietly go to the baby and coach him or her out of the situation. One way to do this is to offer possible suggestions.
◆ Talk about what you see happening: "I see you want that toy back that John took from you. I hear you."
◆ Be at the babies' eye level, and close to the ground where the infants are, and identify what you see.
◆ Speak to both babies who are involved in a situation. "Johnny, you took Mary's toy. Mary doesn't like that. She is crying. I hear you Mary. Johnny took your beads and you are trying to get them, but he still has them. I know you don't like that." Speaking about what is happening to both babies supports each of them without placing blame or judging one or the other.
◆ Intervene with the process or outcome when the safety of one of the babies is at stake. You may have to place your arm between two babies as a boundary to prevent them from hurting one another.
◆ Be available to babies for social and or emotional support as needed.
◆ Provide enough help to babies for them to recognize and solve their problem. "Karina, there is another rattle next to you. Matthew is not willing to give this one up yet."
◆ Identify what the babies may be feeling. For example, "You look frustrated about trying to get down from the slide."
◆ Avoid leaving the scene of the conflict before one of the babies. Being the second one to leave decreases further conflict from happening.
◆ Monitor the play area for short periods (no more than one and a half hours at a time).

When you begin to see that struggling is natural and logical, then the next challenge is what to do when you see struggling occur.

These behaviors need to be practice until they become second nature. When you are able to do some of them, babies will experience their own struggle instead of yours.

Your belief and attitude about the abilities of babies to handle their struggles will influence how babies relate to each other. These beginning social encounters are building blocks to how they will relate to others in their future. Your judgments and values about struggle influence how babies form their attitudes about these encounters. By your careful observation and selective intervention, you can learn to understand the value of struggle as babies gain information and knowledge about their world. So relax, watch, and enjoy.

Key Point

Struggles between babies are natural and positive learning opportunities that develop their social and problem-solving skills. If you monitor struggles in safe ways with babies, you provide a natural outlet for the development of their curiosity, effort, and social skills.

Solutions

◆ Identify your feelings about struggle.
◆ Allow babies to struggle while monitoring their safety.
◆ Talk about exactly what you see happening with the babies.
◆ Remain invested in their process not the outcome.
◆ Keep an open mind about the value of struggle.

Chapter 21

Discovering and Exploring: The Value of Play

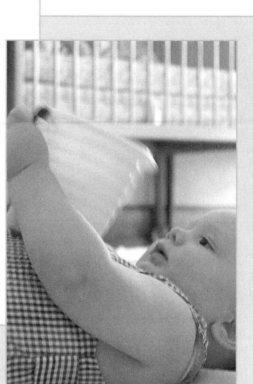

Issue

Play is vital to babies' learning and development. Through play, babies learn important skills that teach them about the world in which they live. Play needs to be valued and seen as opportunities for infants to discover, explore, and be creative.

Rationale

When you see babies at play, you can learn to appreciate, value, and enjoy babies' play experiences. As you watch babies, you will learn that through free play, babies develop their own interests and that babies know intuitively how to play at their level of development and learning. You do not need to teach babies how to play.

Goals

◆ To watch and appreciate babies' free play
◆ To allow babies at the same stage of development to play together
◆ To refrain from teaching babies how to play
◆ To limit the number of babies in the play environment at any given time
◆ To develop safe, appropriate developmental play spaces with varied objects to manipulate
◆ To monitor and maintain play spaces for safety, interest, and needs

Volumes have been written about the value of play. It is one of the most talked-about topics in relation to children. What is really important to know about babies playing? It's important to allow play to happen and that you do not have to teach babies how to play. Babies play to learn how to relate to their world and to figure out how things work. Play is something babies do with their whole bodies. They move, discover, and explore as they grasp, mouth, and manipulate objects. Their play is spontaneous, self-initiated, self-directed, and not goal-oriented. It's as if they *have* to play. When babies are not involved in a caregiving routine, such as diapering, they play, often for long periods when they are not interrupted. When their play is interrupted, their learning is affected.

What you think about babies and about their play will influence what you do (or don't do) when babies play. You may not understand the value and importance of play, and may see play as insignificant and time consuming. A parent was overheard saying to a caregiver, "I took him out of that school because all they did was *play* all day." When a valued caregiver left the child-care field for another job opportunity, a mother said to the caregiver, "Now you'll have a real job and stop playing all day."

You are appreciating and valuing what babies can do when you refrain from teaching them how to play.

Play is simply how babies learn as they interact in their environment; play is an important part of babies' development. While playing, babies interact with objects they choose. Their play is spontaneous, free, and comes from within to express their creativity. There is no "right" or "wrong" way when babies play and, therefore, it does not need to be "corrected." How and with what babies play reflects babies' choices, which need to be honored and respected. Play provides a natural outlet for curiosity and for babies to have social experiences. They develop mastery through play. It is the opportunity by which they work out "struggles" and learn how things work and fit. Play exists for play's sake (Kovach, 1988 as influenced by many conversations with Magda Gerber).

In a local center, the caregiver took three infants between the ages of nine and 13 months, put them in chairs, and without saying a word placed a blank sheet of paper in front of each child. The caregiver then spooned a blob of paint in the center of the paper. Without speaking, the caregiver took each child's hand and made a circular motion, rubbing the paint into the paper. She immediately wrote their names on each of the papers and hung them up to dry. After silently washing each child's hands, she put the babies on the floor.

SCENARIO

Babies in the same compatible stage often play together.

Did these babies play? Did the caregiver support the infants' creativity during this experience? Did she allow free choice? How was the caregiver involved with the babies? Was the experience spontaneous and free or did it come from the adult? These questions will help you to decide whether this is the way you want to be involved with infants during play. In this example, it is obvious that the caregiver created the "art activity" and manipulated the babies during the activity. Maybe her motivation was to give something to the parents at the end of the day, or she may have had to meet the curriculum objectives of that particular program. However, these manipulated exercises do not allow babies to develop their own interests. Play experiences should allow babies to express their natural curiosity and creativity.

So what can play look like with babies who are in a group setting?

◆ First, each baby needs to be in a safe place to move about freely and explore. Magda Gerber discusses a safe environment as one that if the caregiver mistakenly locked herself out of the facility briefly, the babies inside would survive and remain safe, except for a few minor scratches (Gerber & Johnson, 1998). The environment should be totally safe and not rely on the adult to continually safeguard the infants. Of course, this example is only an illustration of how important it is for adults to prepare a safe place for babies to play and explore.

◆ Second, babies need enough space to move about freely and explore on their own. Babies should not be confined in swings, walkers, or other equipment that limits their ability to move and explore.

◆ Third, babies need to be with other babies at the same developmental stage. A rule of thumb is the activity of the baby. For instance, put crawling babies with crawling babies. Placing crawling babies near a baby who cannot move away may be dangerous to that baby. Group size also needs to remain manageable. Observing four or five babies in a play area is enough to watch at one time. One caregiver voiced her concern about how she disliked monitoring the playroom. With nine babies and two adults in the play area, there was too much activity and noise.

When there is more than one caregiver monitoring a play area, frequently the caregivers talk to each other and forget to watch the babies. This can be dangerous for the babies. To improve the above example (nine babies and two adults in a play area), the supervisor and caregivers mutually agreed that a maximum of one adult and five babies in the play area would create a situation that is calm and conducive to play. The play space became more manageable and enjoyable for the caregivers as well as the babies. The smaller group size provided a quiet environment for babies to play and for the caregiver to be more watchful. The caregiver was able to see if the objects and toys were sufficient for the number of babies, and to manage the play area and observe the babies in more meaningful ways.

As you relax, watch, and enjoy babies at play, you begin to value the importance of their play. The following are ways to monitor the play space while babies play:

A watchful caregiver is available to babies without interupting their play.

- ◆ Watch, learn, and appreciate the babies as they play.
- ◆ Sit close to babies, close to or on the ground.
- ◆ Interrupt only for safety reasons or to meet a child's needs.
- ◆ Be available but not interfering.
- ◆ Forget your expectations about how babies should play.
- ◆ Allow an infant to play as long as he or she is happy.
- ◆ Observe the baby's behavior for cues that signal a change (for example, a baby becoming tired).
- ◆ Decide if, when, and how to intervene (see Chapter 19—Providing *Just Enough* Help to Babies on pages 88–92).
- ◆ Let the baby chose his or her own play objects.
- ◆ Tell the baby what you see going on: "I see you have the ball."
- ◆ Refrain from judgments such as, "Good job holding that ball."
- ◆ Reflect instead of praise: "I see you have that ball."
- ◆ Apologize when you need to interrupt the babies' play.

Monitoring babies' play takes effort and energy. Being fully present emotionally is an art that requires practice. Be patient as the babies teach you how to appreciate them. The following are guidelines for the upkeep of the play area, which requires daily tending:

- ◆ Disinfect and replace all small objects every 3–4 hours.
- ◆ Provide a safe play place with indoor and outdoor space for babies to move around in and explore.
- ◆ Insure proper ventilation, lighting, and temperature.
- ◆ Rotate a variety of objects in size, color, shape, and texture.
- ◆ Avoid clutter and too many objects available at one time (set out 2–3 objects per baby).
- ◆ Provide simple objects that babies can grasp and interact with (see Chapter 27 on pages 131–137) safely. Check all objects daily for safety.
- ◆ Make sure there is a play structure for babies to climb; disinfect it daily.
- ◆ Furnish equipment and objects that are child-friendly and are scaled to babies' size.
- ◆ Provide calm and soothing music for short 20-minute intervals (2–3 times a day).

Babies need to play. Play provides a social outlet for babies with many learning opportunities and possibilities. Through play, babies learn to relate to, explore, discover, and problem solve and struggle with objects, as well as to interact with other babies. Your attitude about play influences babies' opportunities for self-discovery. Following the guidelines for a safe play environment will help you to relax and appreciate babies' natural ability during their play. Babies can teach you a lot about play and how to enjoy life through play. You can be part of this amazing experience by allowing babies' play to unfold and honoring each baby's own unique way of play.

Play provides a social outlet that has many learning opportunities and possibilities.

Key Point

Observing babies' play will give you an insight into the importance and need for uninterrupted free play as an expression of babies' discovery and creativity. Allowing babies to play is vital to their total learning process and is not something you need to teach babies to do. Your role is to provide and maintain a safe and developmentally appropriate play environment and to look for signs of the individual needs of babies.

Solutions

◆ Observe babies' play to learn about the importance of babies' free and independent play experiences.
◆ Respect babies' ability to express their uninterrupted free play as vital learning experiences.
◆ Maintain a safe environment that is developmentally interesting with a variety of objects to manipulate.
◆ Maintain play spaces for babies daily to insure a healthy, safe, and interesting play environment.
◆ Allow a small group of babies at the same stage of development to play together.

Chapter 22

Diapering Is a Two-Way Street

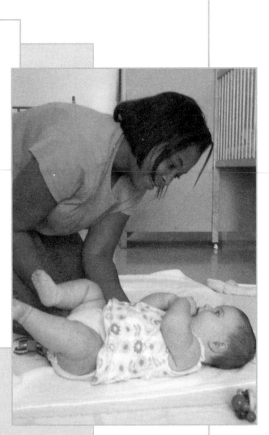

Issue

Diapering is often viewed as a monotonous routine or chore. But, it can be a rich mutual experience that helps to develop a responsive relationship between you and the baby. When diapering is done with cooperative dialogue and interaction between you and the baby, the baby receives the message that he or she is valued.

Rationale

When you respond to babies in social and emotional ways during diapering, pleasurable and meaningful dialogue happens that helps babies understand and participate in what is happening.

Goals

- ◆ To provide a diapering relationship that is rich in dialogue and social-emotional responses between you and the and baby
- ◆ To observe important cues the baby gives to tell you his or her needs
- ◆ To respond to the cues the baby gives in a timely way
- ◆ To design a diapering environment that is efficient and away from interruptions and high-traffic areas

Diapering is a necessary routine that caregivers repeat frequently throughout the day. Each baby in group care needs to be diapered 4–6 times a day, or about 25 times a week. This common event can be a rich and meaningful time together. How rich the diapering event is depends upon your approach with the baby. Your attitude about diapering affects the diapering process with the baby. From the baby's point of view, diapering is a personal body experience that will either be pleasurable or uncomfortable depending on your behavior and responses.

Some caregivers see diapering as a chore, a distasteful task that must be done quickly. Others adults see diapering as a necessary evil that interferes with what they are really supposed to be teaching babies. How often do you hear a caregiver say, "Ooh, let's hurry and get this dirty diaper off so you can play with the toys."

When caring for babies in group care, there are many distractions that interfere with communicating with one specific baby (other babies needing attention, staff interference, noise level). In group care environments, it is difficult to see diapering as an opportunity to spend quality time with a baby. But during the diapering process, there are interactions that are possible that can "refuel" the baby's emotional and social well-being. Consider the following scenarios and the reflection on their differences.

SCENARIO #1

Mary notices a smelly diaper in a nearby crib. She says to her companion caregiver, "Phew! Did you change Chelsea before putting her down?" The other caregiver responds, "No." Mary goes to the infant's crib, picks up the baby, and wordlessly proceeds to change her diaper. During the process of diaper changing, she asks her companion caregiver, "Who else in the room needs to be changed?" After diapering, she puts the baby back in the crib and walks away (Kovach & Da Ros, 1998, p.62).

SCENARIO #2

As Anne, the caregiver, walks by 13-month-old Corina's crib she notices an odor. She stops, looks at Corina, and says, "Corina, I need to pick you up and check your diaper." She extends her hands and waits for the baby's response. After putting Corina on the changing table, she tells Corina exactly what she is going to do before she does it. Anne always gives Corina enough time to respond to her caregiver. Anne spends time diapering Corina, staying focused and attentive to her during the diapering.

These two scenarios are very different. In the first scenario, the caregiver, Mary, does not include Chelsea in her care. By not including Chelsea, the caregiver acts *upon* the baby, giving Chelsea the message that she is an object rather then a person. Mary does not acknowledge Chelsea either by thought or word. This discounts Chelsea as a human being and depersonalizes the caregiving between the two.

In the second example, Anne gets her information directly from Corina beforehand. By including Corina in the diaper-changing process, Anne gives Corina a personal and sensitive diaper change. When Anne includes Corina, she is saying, "You are important enough for my attention." What do these differences suggest? In the first example, Mary gives automated care, which devalues Chelsea. The long-term message is a negative one. It says a baby can be handled without regard. This attitude reinforces passivity in the baby. In the second example, Anne expects Corina to be a part of her care and relies on Corina's reaction during diapering. This shows that Anne thinks Corina's contributions are important, a powerful message to Corina that she is an active part of her life.

Diapering is a two-way street. It is a give-and-take partnership between you and the baby. What you do to support this partnership during diapering is vital to your relationships with the babies in your care. If you want to respond to and support the baby during diapering you need to

◆ Give the baby one-on-one uninterrupted time.
◆ Pay attention and be fully present.
◆ Make eye contact with the baby.
◆ Keep the experience individualized.
◆ Use everyday language, telling the baby what you are going to do before you do it.
◆ Invite the baby to assist in his or her care based on developmental stage.
◆ Move slowly and wait for the baby's response before reacting.
◆ Avoid objects that distract from the diapering process (mirrors, mobiles, toys, and so on).
◆ Stay in the here and now moment.
◆ Touch the baby using sensitive and responsive gestures, such as moving close and being face to face with the baby.

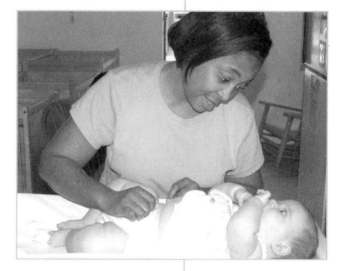

Diapering is a give-and-take partnership.

As you can see, giving the baby your time and undivided attention is essential during diapering. Diapering can offer ample opportunities to engage in meaningful experiences that help develop a trusting relationship. This personalized approach to the baby promotes positive self-esteem (Bettelheim, 1987) and develops the baby's body awareness and social responsiveness (Gerber, 1979). "An infant who is encouraged to actively participate in his or her care will be challenged to master his own care as he grows older" (Gerber, 1979, p. 38). Allowing babies to be included in their care influences how they develop in later life. Your role is essential to the baby's understanding of what is happening. What you do with the baby affects the baby's outlook and ability to master his or her life in later years. What you do with the baby influences how the young child perceives himself now and in his future.

Your beliefs about what babies are capable of and how they should be treated determines your actions in caring for the baby. How much or how little you allow the baby to do influences the activity level of the baby during caregiving. When you allow the baby to participate, the baby will do more on his or her own.

◆ Social and Emotional Responses to Diapering

Although diapering may seem like a chore, it can be a meaningful experience for both you and the baby.

Although diapering may seem like a chore, it can be a meaningful experience for both you and the baby. The goal during diapering is to provide a peaceful time together that is satisfying to both you and the baby. This will allow a relationship to continue to grow and develop. The emotional support you offer the baby during diapering is just as important as physical care. If you forget to wash your hands during diapering, you are responsible for spreading germs and promoting disease. Also, if you forget to show babies they are special, you promote the baby's passivity. Consider the following as you reflect on how to respond emotionally and socially to a baby during the diapering process:

◆ Talk to the baby (about what you are going to do) before changing a diaper. This signals that something is about to happen.

◆ State your observations to the baby while giving care.

◆ Wait for the baby's response. (This give-and-take helps you and the baby understand what is happening. For example, as you wipe the baby's bottom, you notice that the baby flinches. You acknowledge the baby's action by stopping and saying, "I know that is cold on your bottom. I am finished now.")

◆ Talk about what is happening during caregiving. Your mood, tone of voice, touch, and behavior tell the baby what is going on.

◆ Allow the baby to use his or her senses to participate and learn about his or her world. Move slowly. Be fully present and give the baby your undivided attention. This lets the baby know how important he or she is.

By following these simple rules, you include the baby in his or her care, making the diapering process a social activity. When you involve the baby, his or her thoughts and actions become part of the process. These steps allow quality time, which develops a relationship and meets the physical and social-emotional needs of the baby.

◆ The Diapering Place

The diapering place needs to be in a simple, safe, and quiet area away from high-traffic areas. This will minimize disruptions and allow for interactions rich in communication. The diapering area should include the following items:

◆ A stable wooden (preferable) diaper-changing table or area that promotes face-to-face diapering without a lip or boundary around the circumference (This setup insures that the adult places at least one hand on the baby at all times.)

◆ A soft pad for the baby to lie on that can be cleaned and disinfected after each diapering

◆ A sink, preferably with a foot pedal

◆ A tall, lidded diaper can marked "diapers only" with a foot pedal so the caregiver's hands can remain free for the baby

◆ Antibacterial soap for hand washing, disinfectant in a spray bottle for the changing table, and paper towels

◆ A shelf with personal baby items necessary for diapering: diapers, wipes or washcloths, creams, gloves, plastic bags for disposal of soiled diapers, liners if using cloth diapers, and extra set of clothes

The diapering place needs to be a fully equiped, simple, safe area that is set apart from high-traffic areas of the room.

Avoid placing materials in the diaper area that interfere with interactions and personal relationships between babies and caregivers. Toys, mirrors, and mobiles detract the baby from being with you. The diaper area should be a simple, calm, and quiet place. The diaper area should always be in a state of prepared readiness for successful, uninterrupted diapering.

Make sure all items and equipment are readily available for convenience and babies' safety. This will minimize unnecessary interruptions and reflect the high priority you place on the diapering process.

◆ A Respectful Diapering Routine

◆ Move slowly to the baby to be diapered. Bend down with outreached arms and make eye contact with the baby.

◆ Tell the baby what you are going to do before picking him or her up. "Michael, I need to change your diaper. Come." Wait for the baby's response before continuing.

◆ Securely hold the baby for his developmental stage. Very young infants (birth to four or five months) need to have their head and spine supported. For older infants who are able to support their upper trunk, be sure that they can see where they are going while you move to the changing area.

◆ Continue to talk to the baby about what you are doing.

◆ Place the baby on changing table while maintaining eye contact. Keep one hand on the baby at all times.

◆ Avoid restricting the baby's natural movement during diapering. Continue to talk to the baby about what you are doing. Be sure to include your observations to the baby.

◆ Put gloves on and slowly take off the diaper. If it is wet, close the tabs together and place it in the proper container. If it is soiled with feces the rule of thumb in wiping genitals is to move from most clean to dirty. Wipe feces off skin with warm water and a paper towel, or follow your center's procedures. Be sure to wipe down the center of a female baby's vulva first before wiping the right and left side and then front to back. With a male baby, wipe between and around the genitals before wiping front to back. The rule of thumb in wiping genitals is to move from most clean to dirty. Place the soiled diaper in a plastic bag and discard it in the proper container. Continue to tell the baby and show the baby what you are doing. If the baby's bottom is red, take an extra few minutes to clean the baby's bottom, with a sponge if time permits. Water is calming and therapeutic.

◆ Show the baby the clean diaper and allow the baby to feel the diaper before placing it on the baby's body. Show the baby each item of clothing before putting it on his or her body. Encourage and enable the baby to help you dress him or her.

◆ Sit the baby up, if he or she is able to support himself or herself. Wash the baby's hands and face with a warm washcloth while asking for his or her help.

◆ Tell the baby, "Come, it is time to move away from the diaper area." Extend your hands and wait for the baby's response. Pick up the baby securely and transport him or her back to the area where you found him or her. Tell the baby you are leaving to go wash your hands. Slowly move away from the baby. Wash hands turning off faucets with paper towel. Disinfect the changing area.

◆ Record time of urination or bowel movement on the baby's daily information sheet that you share with the baby's family. Note any unusual signs/symptoms observed during diapering. Look over at baby to observe how and what he or she is doing. Does the baby need you to go to him or her, or is he or she content? That observation will determine your next move. (See page 192 in the Appendix for a sample form to record daily diapering, feeding, and activity for each baby.)

◆ Follow regulations outlined in your particular state.

By now you are saying to yourself, "This couldn't happen in the real world. This approach to diapering takes too long." When you use physical care as a time to be really present with the baby, it's easier and more natural and, in the long run, less time consuming because the baby's needs have been met on several developmental levels (physical, emotional, and social). Once you make the commitment to spend quality time with each diapering, you guarantee that each baby has individual time while in group care. This allows the baby to be more satisfied for a longer period of time. Diapering occurs so often for each baby that it's a perfect way to meet the needs of babies in group care.

Key Point

Diapering can be a rich, mutually satisfying experience, which requires a specially equipped area that is away from high-traffic areas. When you involve the baby in the diapering process, you allow the baby to understand what is happening and have an opportunity to cooperate with his or her caregiver.

Solution

◆ Prepare the diaper area ahead of time.
◆ Make sure the diaper-changing area is efficient and effective with no distractions.
◆ Respond to the baby socially and emotionally during diapering.
◆ Maintain a physically safe diapering process.
◆ Provide a one-to-one experience between you and baby that is rich in participation and dialogue.

Chapter 23

Eating: Food For Thought

Issue

Feeding babies, which is a frequent routine, can be delightful and add to your relationship. Or, it can be a necessary, automated routine with little consideration for the physical and emotional needs of the baby.

Rationale

Babies need one consistent primary person who understands their preferences and eating habits. When you observe and respond to babies' signals during feedings times, you are able to meet their needs. When you know and are responsive to each baby's needs and preferences, you can help them learn what his or her body is saying. Also, creating predictable eating routines helps babies know what to expect. This allows the baby to trust you.

Goals

- ◆ To assign a primary caregiver to feed the same baby throughout the day
- ◆ To provide an efficient and quiet space for eating that is away from high-traffic areas
- ◆ To set up feeding routines that the baby can rely on

Food is a very personal issue. Preferences for how and what we eat develop as early as infancy. How adults feed and relate with babies while they eat affects their nutrition and future choices.

Having a philosophy and rationale about how to feed babies is vital to their general health. The philosophy needs to consider babies' physical and emotional well-being while eating.

Infants have tiny stomachs, so they need smaller amounts of food more frequently. Because of this, young babies need to learn how to interpret their cues for eating. You can help the baby begin to learn about his or her body and how much food he or she needs to be satisfied. Do this by observing babies during feeding time while giving the babies enough time to eat. It is easy to rush through feeding babies. When this happens, babies can get stomachaches, gas problems, or spit up food or formula. Babies need a lot of time to eat to satisfaction, usually 20–30 minutes at each feeding. It is easy to misinterpret when the baby is satisfied. Babies rest between ounces of formula and helpings of food. Caregivers may interpret this as a signal that the baby is finished eating.

Young babies who drink one to two ounces often will drift off to sleep for a short period of time. Sitting the baby up to burp at that time may bring the baby to a more awake state. Talking to the baby also helps the baby to stay awake. He then may be ready for more food. Babies in the first year of life generally need 28–32 ounces of formula during a 24-hour period of time. Also, very young babies (two to three months) may initially eat 2–3 ounces every two and a half to three hours until they become a little older (say three and a half to four months). Getting to know a baby's eating habits and recording them daily will create a pattern to guide you. Families are valuable sources of information about their baby's eating habits. It is very important to ask parents or families what patterns of eating already exist. Feeding babies in familiar ways helps babies be more comfortable with their caregiver.

Young infants should be held by a familiar adult at each feeding (whether bottle or solids). This is especially important in center-based care. Paying special attention to each baby's need is important to understanding food preferences. When you pay attention to babies' choices, you help them develop preferences. This is important because babies spend many hours in group care and need nourishment to grow and develop.

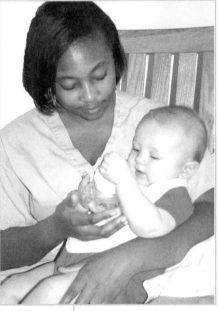

In center-based care, caregivers may become anxious that there is not enough time to feed each baby in a slow and leisurely manner. But spending quality time during feeding often meets babies' physical and emotional needs. When this happens, babies are content to explore and play on their own. If the

Babies' needs are more apt to be met when they are held by familiar adults.

needs of babies are met during caregiving times, they will be content to be on their own at other times. This will give caregivers time to devote to the individual needs of all babies.

The manufacturers of baby furniture heard the plea of "I have no time to feed all the babies" and created a five-compartment group feeding table for caregivers' convenience. A consultant in infant care relays a story often seen in child care centers: In one visit, she noted five mobile infants each sitting in one of the compartment seats being fed in rapid succession by a well-meaning, frazzled caregiver. The consultant paid particular attention to the "story" told by the expressions on the infants' faces. One was trying to stay awake with cereal on most of his face. One baby was crying loudly, and one baby was slouched over in discomfort. The director apologized to the consultant for the caregiver who was not feeding the babies efficiently enough. The consultant's response was, "Under the circumstances, she is doing a better job than I could. There is no way I could feed five babies at one time and make them all happy."

Because the baby is the curriculum and food is a vital part of the baby's ability to thrive, what better way to spend time with the baby than during his or her feeding times!

Because the baby is the curriculum and food is a vital part of the baby's ability to thrive, what better way to spend time with the baby than during his or her feeding times! To individualize feeding times, infants need time and people available to give that time. Ticking watches do not belong in the baby room. *Time is to be given, not looked at.*

When feeding babies, following certain principles will help develop their healthy eating habits:
◆ Food is nourishment.
◆ Eating should be a pleasurable experience.
◆ Encourage babies to participate during eating and control the amount of food they eat.
◆ Create a philosophy and predictable routine for eating and feeding.
◆ Provide a specific calm place for eating that is away from high-traffic areas.
◆ Eating involves the baby's sense of taste, smell, touch, sight, and hearing.
◆ Eating is developmental. The baby needs to be able to demonstrate his or her ability and preferences as he or she grows and develops.
◆ The environment needs to work for you and the baby. Are the equipment and furniture available and child friendly? Can the baby get in and out on his or her own if he or she is able?
◆ You and the infant need to sit together. A baby who cannot sit up on his or her own needs to be fed on your lap. Babies who sit up on their own can be at a small table with you sitting across from him or her to offer assistance as needed.

If you support the baby's abilities for bottle and solid feeding, you strengthen the infant's independence and competence. Knowing how much the baby can do on his or her own and allowing the baby to experience independence and competence during eating is basic to the baby's learning. It is through trial and error that he or she gains competence.

Babies drink 4–6 bottles a day and are in group care for many of these bottle feedings. The way in which each baby gets to drink from the bottle is important. You need to be consistent in how you offer the bottle to each baby. Techniques for bottle feeding include the following:

◆ Watch for cues that the baby is hungry. Talk to the baby about whether he or she wants to eat.

◆ Wash your hands and get the baby's bottle ready while telling the baby what you are doing. You may want to include the baby in his bottle preparation by having him nearby or holding him while his milk is warming in the crock pot. If you decide to include the baby, do so every time consistently.

◆ Sit with the baby in a comfortable chair with a firm back at the designated eating area. Get in a comfortable position. You may need to support your elbow with a small pillow to ease stress from the weight of the baby's head. The baby's body should be lying in your arms at about a 45-degree angle.

◆ Show the baby the bottle and make eye contact. Talk to him or her about what you are doing. Put the nipple to his or her lips and wait for the baby to take the nipple in his or her mouth and suck. Look at the baby's face from time to time. Try not to make continual eye contact or speak to the baby for the entire time while he or she is sucking because babies stop sucking to listen to your voice. Talk to the baby when you are burping him or her. Make sure the baby's hands are free.

◆ Hold the bottle for very young babies. As the baby develops, he or she will grasp the bottle. Many babies hold the end of the bottle for brief periods. Eventually, the baby will hold his or her own bottle. When the baby takes more responsibility for holding the bottle, lighten your grasp on the bottle.

◆ Let the baby have as much as he or she wants to drink. If the baby turns away or shows disinterest, do not force the baby to eat or continue to try to feed the baby. Observe and respect the baby's needs. It usually takes 20–30 minutes to feed a baby a bottle. Many young babies fall asleep for brief periods of time while sucking a bottle. Gently sit the baby up to burp or softly talk to the baby. Putting a baby to sleep is not the purpose of bottle-feeding.

◆ Burping babies can be done in several subtle ways. Sitting the baby at a 45-degree angle is sufficient to allow the baby to burp. Holding the baby up and against your chest is also another way to help baby burp. Be sure to support his or her head and neck and keep his or her feet off your lap so the baby will not put weight on his or her feet.

◆ When the baby seems uninterested in drinking more, wait and ask the baby if he or she is finished. Babies give cues that they are done when they stop sucking, push bottle away, or turn their head and/or try to sit up.

◆ Slowly move the baby from the eating area to the play area or his or her crib, or change his or her diaper, depending on the baby's needs.

Feeding babies their bottle can be a source of pleasure and satisfaction for both you and the baby.

Feeding babies their bottle can be a source of pleasure and satisfaction for both you and the baby. By giving babies enough quality time, both you and the baby can be "refueled." Consider this situation between the caregiver and baby.

Estelle enjoys leisurely feeding of Marion. While on her lap, she watches Marion's cues that help her understand how the baby is doing and what she needs. When Estelle is done feeding Marion, she calmly sits and waits for Marion to burp. Estelle is not in any hurry to rush to her next chore. She sits and enjoys a few minutes of being with Marion. Marion relaxes in her caregiver's arms and looks up as she smiles at Estelle. Baby Marion is probably feeling unrushed, nurtured, and accepted by her interactions and relationship with Estelle.

Equipment needed for bottle feeding:

◆ Good, steady, and comfortable supportive chair
◆ Bottle, washcloth, bib
◆ Burp cloth
◆ Quiet area away from high traffic

Guidelines for feeding babies who are able to sit up and support their upper bodies on their own include the following. Babies are ready to sit at a child-sized table and stool when they:

◆ Are able to support his head, neck, and upper body
◆ Start cutting teeth
◆ Have control of hands
◆ Are creeping and crawling
◆ Show strong interest in what goes on in the world around him
◆ Show interest in food when you eat
◆ Are able to sit on a stool with feet on the floor

Eating is a pleasurable experience when babies and caregivers are working together.

Guidelines for the process of babies eating solids sitting at the table and chair:

◆ Have the food tray prepared and the table set.
◆ Tell the baby you have his or her food ready.
◆ Help the baby to the table, allowing him or her to move toward without your help. (For example, if he or she can crawl to table, don't carry the baby.)
◆ Show the stool to the baby and help him or her sit, if necessary; make sure the baby's feet are on the floor for balance; sit across or to the side of the baby.
◆ Show the baby the bib and let him or her touch it before you put it on him.
◆ Show the food to the baby.
◆ Have a spoon available.
◆ Fill a spoon half full of food and bring it to the baby's eye level. Say the name of the food.
◆ Bring the spoon to the baby's lip.

- Wait for the baby to open his or her mouth.
- Let the baby initiate bringing food into his or her mouth.
- Repeat until baby gives a cue that he or she no longer wants more food.
- Pour liquid slowly in an unbreakable glass, allowing the baby to see and hear liquid going into the glass.
- Bring the glass to the baby's mouth, if the baby is unable to hold the glass.
- Allow the baby to leave the table when ready. Offer a wet washcloth to wipe his or her face, and ask the baby to put his or her hands in washcloth. Say, "Give me your hand," and gently touch the hand you are asking for. Over time, the baby will give you his or her hand.
- Take off the bib and allow the baby to leave the table on his or her own, if he or she is able. Otherwise, help the baby to the floor to crawl away.

Equipment needed for babies eating sitting up:
- Child-size table and chairs (wood is preferable)
- Child-size stool (wood is preferable)
- Clear plastic bowl used for food (so baby can see the substance in bowl)
- Small clear plastic glass (large enough to hold one to two ounces of liquid)
- Two small-bowled spoons for you and the baby
- Bib
- Washcloth
- Small tray to hold bowl and other eating utensils

Eating at a small table with stools allows you and the baby to participate and cooperate. It offers the baby choice, preference, and an opportunity to use his or her skills. It also supports the baby's independence. It allows the baby control over what goes into his or her body and how much food he or she needs to be satisfied. Serve food in small amounts and offer frequent helpings. This technique allow the baby to be more involved in deciding how much to eat. In this way, the baby is not overwhelmed by large amounts of food on his or her plate at one time. When a baby sits at his own table and stool, he learns to maintain balance on his own. He can decide when to leave the table. This way of eating develops the child's initiation and self-regulation.

Allowing babies to decide how much to eat helps them learn what their bodies need.

Feeding babies is one of the most important tasks that you do. Lifelong attitudes about food, nourishment, social, and self-help skills start in infancy. You are instrumental in developing babies' healthy food habits in this early stage of development.

It is essential to prepare the eating area, observe baby's cues while he or she is eating, and be available while the baby is eating for the baby to have a successful eating experience. The baby needs your full attention and concentration so you can learn when and how to help during eating by reading the baby's cues and signals. Learning these signals helps you develop successful eating routines and reinforce babies' participation. Your belief in the baby's ability encourages the baby to learn and develop skills while eating.

Your belief in the baby's ability to feed herself encourages her to develop eating skills.

Key Point

When the same primary caregiver always observes and responds to a baby's signals during feeding, the baby has a more fulfilled eating experience. Paying attention to babies' responses helps you understand their preferences and habits. This can help you create routines. Reliable routines help babies understand what to expect and aid their participation during feeding. Designing effective eating space in quiet areas also supports individual and peaceful time for babies while they eat.

Solutions

- ◆ Assign caregivers to feed the same infants every day.
- ◆ Allow time for you and the baby to enjoy a pleasurable eating experience.
- ◆ Design a quiet area that is fully functional for eating success.
- ◆ Be consistent and predictable in the routine you develop for the baby's eating experiences.

Chapter 24

Rest Stop

Issue

Babies need sleep routines that they can count on to insure proper rest. In today's busy world, babies often do not have regular sleep patterns and routines. You can be helpful by responding to the cues babies give when they are tired.

Rationale

When babies are tired, they need to rest peacefully in a familiar place. Helping babies develop healthy sleep patterns requires accurate and timely observation by caregivers. When you respond to babies with consistent routines that they can rely on, babies are more comfortable.

Goals

◆ To adjust schedules to fit babies' sleep needs
◆ To accurately read and respond to signals that babies are tired
◆ To create designated sleep spaces
◆ To create consistent, predictable sleep routines

Helping babies to develop good sleep habits is a major issue for both parents and caregivers. Babies are aware that the infant room is different from their home space and may have distractions, such as noise, people moving around, and other babies needing care. Each baby has to learn to adjust to these differences in order to be calm enough to fall asleep. Creating sleep routines that the baby can rely on may require asking families what has worked for them at home. Their information can be helpful in the baby's adjustment to sleeping at the center.

It is helpful to watch for soft signs of tiredness, such as the baby becoming inactive or showing signs of irritability. When this occurs, tell the baby before he or she falls asleep that you are going to put him or her in bed.

If you are insensitive to the need babies have for sleep, it affects the babies' ability to develop good sleep habits. They don't learn to sense when their bodies need rest. This can impact your ability to help babies fall asleep.

When babies have created patterns of sleep, they are able to adjust to routines of sleep in center care. Caregivers often feel pressure and frustration in regard to helping babies fall asleep and may have to make adjustments based on what the baby is already used to. For more detailed reading on sleep refer to specific chapters in Gerber's book *Dear Parent* (1998) and Gonzalez-Mena and Eyer's book *Infants, Toddlers, and Caregivers: A Curriculum of Respectful, Responsive Care and Education* (2004). These books offer suggestions on how to develop healthy sleep patterns for babies.

Reading babies' cues helps them fall asleep on their own. Providing sleep spaces for each baby supports this process.

Babies should be able to sleep on their own according to their own body rhythm. Don't assume a group of babies will need to sleep at the same time. Each baby's need for rest varies and each baby expresses his or her need to rest differently. Observant caregivers learn the individual sleep patterns of each baby and when these sleep patterns change. These sensitive observations help to interpret a baby's signals, which can range from subtle yawning to irritability or emotional frustration and crying.

When you read babies' sleep cues (yawning, eye rubbing, quiet, red eyes, crying, pulling ears, inactivity) promptly and accurately, you will be able to place the baby in bed before the baby falls asleep. Below are two distinct scenarios featuring caregivers who react differently based on their observations. Decide which caregiver appears to be more sensitive in meeting the baby's need.

Karesha, the caregiver in an infant room, just finished feeding six-month-old Jamie. She places him on a blanket on the floor with several interesting toys nearby. After 15 minutes, Karesha notices Jamie yawning a few times. She makes a mental note to check on him later. Thirty minutes later Karesha watches as Jamie dozes in the play area. When she goes to get him, she notices his eyes are closed. Karesha decides not to move Jamie to his crib as he might awaken, cry, and lose his chance for sleep.

Yolanda has just finished feeding Bryson, an eight-month-old and places him near another baby of the same compatible stage. That is, both babies can function at about the same level of development. Bryson is on a blanket on the floor with several objects nearby to grasp. After 20 minutes, Bryson begins to yawn and blink his eyes. Yolanda notices Bryson seems disinterested in his present surroundings and is beginning to get inactive. She moves to where Bryson is and says to him, "I am going to pick you up and put you in your crib for your rest."

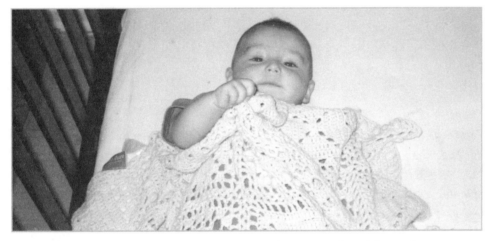

The watchful eye of a caregiver helps babies feel content when falling asleep.

Each of the caregivers, Karesha and Yolanda, observed cues from the babies about being tired. Each caregiver responded based on her observation. Karesha was a little late responding to her observation and left Jamie on the floor to sleep. On the other hand, Yolanda observed early signs of Bryson being tired and offered him an opportunity to rest before he became overtired. The main difference between the two caregivers is that Yolanda was able to observe and interpret Bryson's cues in a timely way that allowed him to sleep peacefully in his own bed. When Karesha missed Jamie's initial cues, he fell asleep on the floor. By the time she noticed Jamie asleep, she didn't want to risk moving him. Observing and reading cues accurately and in a timely fashion is essential to responsive caregiving.

Information about the baby's sleep pattern is important to understanding how to put babies to sleep in center care. Families know what does and does not work for their baby. It helps to develop a working relationship with the families of the babies in your care. Families are valuable sources of information about their babies' likes and dislikes. They can offer assistance on what has and hasn't worked and can help by describing the baby's routines. Specific, daily communication, such as how the baby slept the night before, is valuable to help you understand the baby's rest needs while at the center.

It is often a very difficult task for caregivers to nap babies who are in group care. The following attitude and action guidelines will help caregivers to create restful sleep patterns for babies:

◆ Believe each baby has his or her own unique preferences and sleep needs.
◆ Provide a consistent, peaceful sleep space for each baby.
◆ Trust that the baby will sleep when tired.
◆ Create consistent routines for sleep (first you eat, then play, and then sleep).
◆ Respond to cues when the baby appears tired.
◆ Use the sleep space only for naps.
◆ Adopt an attitude about the baby's ability to develop self-soothing behaviors. Avoid using back rub, rocking, and singing lullabies that tell the baby that he or she needs help to sleep.

SCENARIO

Marty was a lead teacher for a group of eight older babies around 11–14 months old. These babies were able to sit up, creep, and crawl and some could stand and walk. After a few weeks, Marty came to her supervisor because she was having difficulty putting her babies to sleep. Marty was trying to nap all the babies at one time and found out that her babies were not sleeping. By early afternoon, the babies were miserable—tired, cranky, and whiny. Marty was miserable, too, and often had a headache by 2:00 p.m.

After a lengthy discussion with her supervisor, Marty decided to try a different approach to sleep, one that is based on each baby's individual need for rest. She utilized the room designating a space for physical care (eating, diapering, sleeping) and using another part of the room as a play space. Marty assigned her assistant, Danielle, to monitor the play area. Marty decided to take responsibility for the babies' sleep routines. She based her actions on her observations of the babies.

Before going out to the play area, Marty prepared the nap area for sleep. She placed each baby's mat down on the floor wherever they were used to sleeping and put their individual blanket on their mat. Marty turned off the lights in the sleeping area. Whenever Marty noticed a baby showing signs of tiredness, she moved to the child at eye level and extended her hands saying, "You look tired. It's time for your rest." She then helped the baby to the nap area. Slowly, Marty guided the baby to her mat and after showing the baby the blanket, covered the child saying, "You have a nice rest," before moving away. She repeated these steps with each baby who showed signs of being tired. This kind of care plan involved Marty adjusting her attitude and the schedule to fit each baby's sleep needs. Marty's decision paid off when she was able to see and feel how happy and peaceful the babies were after their nap.

◆ Sleep Space Design

Babies need a special rest area that is just for sleep. An environment that is properly prepared is essential for successful sleep. These preparations include providing:
- Soft natural light
- A room temperature that is not too cold or too warm
- Consistent sleep space with no distracting objects
- An attitude that supports the notion that sleep is a natural body function
- A quiet, calm, and peaceful atmosphere
- Enough time for babies to develop their own self-soothing techniques
- Time to observe babies' cues about tiredness
- An individual crib, futon, mattress, or mat for each infant
- Personal blankets and nonrestrictive clothing
- Assurance that the baby's physical needs have been met
- Predictable routines that include sleep as a part of the sequence

Babies' sleep spaces need to be clean and simple. They also need to be separate fron other areas in the room.

Preparing the sleep space helps promote sleep for babies in group care. Steps to transitioning an infant to the sleep area include the following:
- Observe the baby for beginning signs of tiredness (check to see when the last nap, feeding, and diaper change occurred).
- Go to the baby and say, "You look a little tired. Come [extend hands]. Let me put you in your bed."
- Pick up the baby, supporting head, neck, and spine.
- Securely hold the baby and allow the baby to see where you are taking him or her.
- Offer a drink if you think the baby is thirsty.
- Tell the baby you are putting him or her in bed and place him or her on his or her back.
- Show the baby the blanket. Let him or her feel it, and very softly tell him or

her it's time to rest. Do not hesitate, or get into a dialogue. The baby will become confused about what you expect of him or her. If the baby cries after you put him in his crib, try to find out what the baby is saying by the cry. Some babies cry before they fall asleep. You have to get to know your babies to understand the "why" of the cry.

◆ If the baby is not asleep in 10 minutes, ask the baby if he or she wants to come out of his or her crib.

Note: Leaving babies in cribs for long periods of time when they are awake is confusing for them and under-stimulating. If the baby does not fall asleep, try again later when he or she appears to be tired.

The goal of sleep is to provide rest when babies need it, which allows them to develop healthy sleep habits. Through your observations and responses you can help the baby understand when his or her body needs rest. Babies often give cues when they begin to feel tired. Some signs of tiredness include the following:

◆ Rubbing eyes
◆ Sucking fingers, thumb, or fist
◆ Pulling on ears
◆ Yawning
◆ Red eyes

◆ Crying
◆ Rubbing head
◆ Closing eyes
◆ Less movement

Key Point

Babies rest better when they are tired and when you observe and respond to their cues quickly. Having a consistent sleep routine and sleeping in one's own familiar space provides security for babies and helps them learn how to regulate their own bodies for sleep.

Solutions

◆ Observe and respond to each baby's sleep cues before he or she shows signs of being overtired.
◆ Provide a sleep space that is quiet and away from other activities.
◆ Be aware of previous patterns of sleep.
◆ Create a routine of sleep babies get to know and understand.
◆ Make sure babies' physical care needs are met before sleep.
◆ Always put the baby to sleep in his or her own sleep space.
◆ Let the baby know he or she is going to rest before falling asleep.
◆ Keep a positive attitude about babies' ability to regulate their own body for sleep.

Chapter 25

Learn to Move, Move To Learn

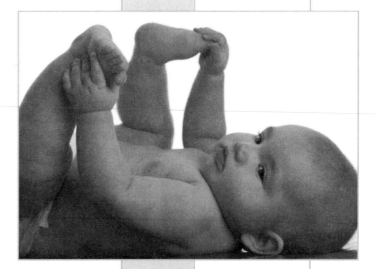

Issue

Babies move when they are ready and in their own way. When you rush babies to sit before they are able or restrict babies' movements by placing them in swings or seats, it prevents them from learning motor skills at their own pace and affects their sense of balance.

Rationale

Babies need to move freely in a safe place. When babies are allowed to move and explore on their own, they learn about their environment and their abilities. Babies develop confidence and problem-solving skills as they move, explore, and relate to their environment.

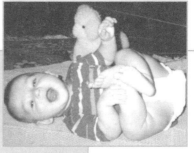

Goals

◆ To allow babies to move freely on their own timetable and in their own way
◆ To avoid placing babies in positions they are not ready to get in and out of on their own

Babies are happy and content to move freely on their own.

Roxanne finished diapering 13-month-old Sierra. Roxanne picked up Sierra from the changing table, carried her over to the high chair, and strapped her in. After feeding Sierra, the caregiver carried her to a swing and placed her in the swing. The swing rocked as the music played. After 30 minutes of swinging, Sierra fell asleep. Instead of putting Sierra in her crib, Roxanne decided not to disturb the napping baby and left her sleeping in the swing.

Well-meaning caregivers working with young infants often carry babies around from one area to another and use equipment, like a swing, to soothe them. The end result is that babies miss opportunities to engage in free movement, which decreases babies' opportunities to participate in and experience their world. In the above example, Roxanne's attitude about what babies can and should do and her resulting behavior limited Sierra's opportunities to move and experience what she can do with her body. She was not able to actively explore and discover her world. Restricting Sierra's freedom of movement may also communicate to Sierra that she should not try to move, which weakens her confidence.

You have the opportunity to allow babies to move and explore their bodies based on their own physical capabilities. The best position for a newborn baby is on his or her back because it allows the baby to move freely, given his or her stage of development. Babies do not need to be placed on their stomach. They will roll over on the tummy when they are ready. When they do so, they are able to lift their heads. Magda Gerber stated frequently, "We need to respect what infants can do instead of encouraging them to do what they are not ready to do" (Gerber & Johnson, 1998, p. 53). The *way* in which an infant moves instinctively is more important than *when* he moves. Each baby needs to develop at his or her own rate. Allowing babies to move when they are ready is the best way for them to develop their gross motor abilities. Putting or propping babies in positions that they cannot support physically or emotionally is not the best way for babies to develop.

Placing young babies on their backs allows them to move freely.

This brings to mind the mother who came for an interview with her mobile infant. The mother clearly stated that Eric "sits up on his own," a skill that was required for acceptance into the infant room, which had one opening left. During the evaluation meeting with the mother and Eric, the director noticed that the mother placed Eric in a sitting position. Eric began to wobble and eventually fell sideways to the floor. The director asked Eric's mom, "Is it okay to leave Eric on his back to see if he sits up on his own?" Mom replied, "Oh, he can't get into a sitting position by himself. He only stays sitting once I put him in that position." Mom's dilemma was that she wanted Eric to sit up so he could be accepted into the room that had the opening. However, Eric was unable to support a sitting position on his own.

Babies move for the pure pleasure of moving. They have to move! Babies flourish in their physical development, including the quality of their movements and their sense of judgment, when you allow them to move freely at their own pace. For this to happen, the key element is time.

When ready, babies achieve their own sense of balance.

The way a baby moves naturally and instinctively is always the safest way for him or her. The best way that you can help is to allow the baby the freedom to move in his or her own way and at his or her own pace. Sometimes that means sitting on your hands and developing a little faith in the baby. But by doing so, you allow infants to gain their own sense of balance. For the infant, gaining balance is necessary for secure movement. A noted authority on gross motor development, Dr. Emmi Pikler, stated, "an infant who was allowed to move freely could 'practice' the skills needed to progress to the next stage of development. For example, a baby who couldn't sit wouldn't be propped with pillows into a sitting position. By lying on his back, moving his arms and legs, and rolling to his side, he would naturally strengthen the muscles and develop the coordination needed to sit" (Gerber & Johnson, 1998, p. 14).

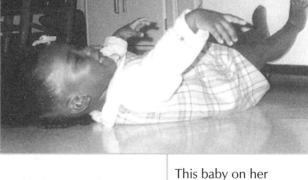

This baby on her back can develop and strengthen her coordination through practice.

Do not interfere with the baby's movement unless it is unsafe. By using the following simple guidelines, you will help the baby to gain balance, skill, and competence while he or she moves:

◆ Have faith that babies know instinctively how to move the best way for them at a particular time.
◆ Re-evaluate your thinking about helping a "helpless" baby get into a position he or she may not be ready to support.
◆ Restrict the space to move, not babies' movements.
◆ Dress babies in comfortable, nonrestrictive clothing, using the least amount of clothing while still being dressed appropriately for the weather.
◆ Allow babies to be shoeless indoors for their first year. Babies need their toes for balance.
◆ Avoid walking aids and pieces of equipment that restrict movement, such as swings, infant seats, bouncers, and activity gyms.
◆ Carry babies in respectful ways.

- Set up a safe environment that has interesting objects (see Chapter XX) that help babies develop their physical skills.
- Observe, appreciate babies' movements, and interfere as little as possible.

Dr. Emmi Pikler (Gerber, 1979, p. 62) studied 720 children to understand how children learned motor skills through their own self-induced movements. The study showed that babies who were allowed to move freely and to practice moving moved more independently. These babies were more able to change positions earlier. They did not expect help from adults. Once you embrace and apply these facts, you will develop confidence in letting babies move on their own. Trust comes with knowledge and practice. The more you see and observe babies' capabilities, the more you will trust in what they can do on their own.

Key Point

Babies move instinctively in ways that are safe for them. If you allow babies to move when they are ready and in their own way, you will support babies' natural ability and promote their self-exploration and learning. Babies who are allowed to gain balance on their own develop confidence in their movements. As babies repeat movements, they perfect the quality of their movements.

Solutions

- Provide a safe place for babies to move and explore their environment.
- Allow babies to move in their own time and in their own way.
- Avoid placing babies in equipment that restricts their mobility.
- Place young infants on their backs as a beginning position.

Babies need a safe place to move around in when exploring and learning about their environment.

Chapter 26

Speak *to* Not *at:* Supporting Babies' Language Development

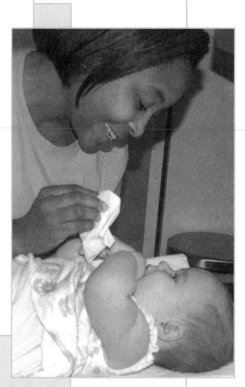

Issue

Language is a powerful tool that babies rely on to learn about and understand what is happening. What you say to them matters to their learning and development.

Rationale

Babies need many opportunities to hear and be exposed to language. Babies need you to talk to and with them about what is happening. When you provide a language-rich environment for babies, they have a better chance to understand what is taking place.

Goals

- ◆ To talk *to* babies, not *at* them
- ◆ To provide many language-rich opportunities throughout the day
- ◆ To refrain from talking about babies in their presence
- ◆ To clearly express verbal and nonverbal language to the baby
- ◆ To use language to reflect what is happening to babies

Language is communication. In one of her videos about babies (*Seeing Infants with New Eyes*), leading infant authority, Magda Gerber stated, "Many people talk better to their dogs than their children." While this may not be true for everyone, you may have been in situations where you see adults handle babies without talking to them. You have also seen adults talking to babies in high-pitched voices. Maybe you speak in these ways to try to get the baby's attention. Maybe you don't realize babies are acute observers. So it is not necessary for adults to call attention to babies with a lot of noise and hoopla (Caulfield, 1995; Tizard, Cooperman, Joseph, & Tizard, 1972). These behaviors suggest that babies need extra effort to pay attention to adults. Much of these exaggerated efforts to get the baby's attention are learned by adults. Research studies have also contributed to this idea of getting babies' attention (Howes, 1998; Kovach & Da Ros, 1995; Lally & Mangione, 2006).

Another behavior that devalues babies is talking *about* babies instead of *to* them in their presence. Where did you learn to do this? Adults don't talk to other adults in this manner (at least, we hope they don't!). Some caregivers might do this because they were taught in the past that babies learn much later in life than they do.

What about you? Do you talk to babies when you are with them or caring for them? If not, why not? Maybe talking to babies about what you are doing with them feels odd and unfamiliar to you. If that is so, you are not alone. Consider the following example: A caregiver was trying to talk to a baby and tell the baby that she was going to pick her up. The caregiver's actions and speech did not match. She picked the baby up and added as an afterthought, "I'm going to pick you up now." It can feel awkward talking to babies about what you are doing. It requires practice to feel at ease if you are not used to it. However, telling babies what you are doing gives them important information they need in order to respond. Taking time to do this means you have to slow down and develop patience. However, if, over time, you talk with babies about what you are doing, you provide social-emotional experiences that create and develop a relationship between you and the baby. Watch the baby's reaction as you talk; maybe the baby's responses will convince you to support language with your babies.

There are different ways to communicate with babies depending on the situation:

◆ Talk to babies to give them information about what is happening.
◆ Talk to babies to reflect on what you see.
◆ Sportscast to babies (describe what you see).
◆ Respond to the baby's reaction to you.
◆ Make sure your verbal and nonverbal language clearly give the same message.

Talk to babies to give them information about what is happening.

Can you think of other ways you can communicate with the babies in your care? First, tell the baby what you are going to do. Then, wait for the baby's response. Be sure to include the baby's response in your next verbal message. For example, Glenda says, "Come Chad, I want to pick you up now." Chad turns his face and body away from the caregiver. Glenda observes these valuable cues and replies, "I know you may not want me to pick you up, but I need to change your diaper." What Glenda did in her second verbal message was to recognize and respond to Chad's turning away. Babies' nonverbal body cues are important to recognize as part of communication. Through these cues, information is given to assess and understand the baby's point of view before responding. Glenda picked up on Chad's cue and included it in her dialogue with him. Glenda's message includes the baby, his feelings, and his reactions—an important ingredient to babies' communication and mutual understanding.

Sportscasting is another way of communicating with babies. Sportscasting is when you verbally reflect on your observations and include your observations in your dialogue with the baby. For example, two babies, around the same age, were playing nearby on the floor. Trevor was manipulating a rattle. Elisa took the rattle from Trevor. Trevor cried and looked over to the caregiver. The caregiver responded to Trevor, "I saw that she took your rattle, I know that makes you unhappy." The message given by the caregiver here is that she is nearby watching, listening, and responding. Acknowledging the infant's actions and feelings in a nonjudgmental way helps babies feel understood. Because infants learn through experiences with others, it is important to them to hear the language of their culture from a responsive adult. The more the baby is exposed to everyday language, such as words that label objects or describe things or actions, the more the baby will absorb and develop language skills. Using language is an "insurance policy" to stay emotionally and socially connected to the baby.

The more the baby is exposed to everyday language, such as words that label objects or describe things or actions, the more the baby will absorb and develop language skills.

When you use language with a baby, it
◆ indicates that you are interested;
◆ demonstrates that you respect the baby as an individual;
◆ shows the baby that you are trying to understand and learn about what he or she is trying to communicate;
◆ provides you and the baby with ongoing opportunities to better understand each other;
◆ helps keep the experience in the here and now, the present moment;
◆ insures a dialogue between you and the baby where you are responding to one another;
◆ demonstrates that you acknowledge the baby as more than an object; and
◆ helps you and the baby to anticipate and respond to each other's cues.

Language links meaning and understanding.

Acknowledging the importance of language demonstrates your critical role in talking to and accurately responding to the baby. The message about language is strong and clear. Talk *with* not *at* the babies in your care. Language is your link between action and meaning. When you talk to babies, they begin to understand better what you are asking and doing. The baby then can gain information and anticipate what will come to be expected. When you support babies in this way, language is not only a tool to understanding but also a way to show babies respect.

Key Point

When babies are allowed to experience language as a part of their culture, they make meaningful connections to help them understand what is happening. You are the key to helping babies make those connections when you speak with them, describe actions and things, and use gestures that provide them with important signals and information.

Solutions

◆ Spend time talking with babies.
◆ Use caregiving routines to help babies make those communication connections.
◆ Make sure your verbal and nonverbal responses say the same thing to babies.
◆ Include the baby when talking with other adults.
◆ Use single-word sentences to talk to young babies.
◆ Describe, reflect, and label to help babies make connections.
◆ Include your observations with babies in your dialogue together.
◆ Make social and emotional connections with babies through your language experience.

Chapter 27

Objects: Not Too Many and Not too Few

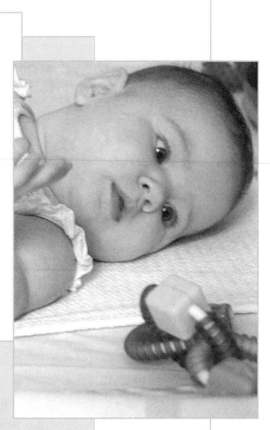

Issue

There are many objects that you can chose to offer babies for their play. Toy companies create playthings that are multicolored and have functions that require little interaction on the part of the baby. However, babies' brains develop by relating to objects in ways that develop their interest, curiosity, problem-solving skills, and sensory experiences. You may be wooed by marketing strategies to buy too many complex playthings for babies. However, too much stimulation at one time can confuse and cause babies to miss potential learning experiences.

Rationale

Babies don't need to be entertained by objects that overstimulate their senses. Instead, they need time to explore simple objects. Their experiences become more complex as babies grow and develop. When babies manipulate objects, they learn the different properties and functions of the objects. When babies are overstimulated and entertained by objects and toys, they tend to become passive onlookers instead of active learners.

Goals

◆ To choose basic, simple toys that babies can actively explore and interact with

◆ To allow babies to use their hands as learning tools to grasp and manipulate objects in their environment

◆ To provide a variety of objects that have different properties (soft, mouthed, non-toxic, colorful, textured, wheeled) and functions (roll, stack, bounce) that babies can choose in their play

◆ To decrease chaos and excessive stimulation in babies' play spaces

◆ To maintain an orderly environment that allows babies to develop their skills and concentration

◆ To refrain from teaching babies how to play and, instead, to observe babies' active involvement in their play experience

Billions and billions of dollars are spent on toys for children. Toys are meant to keep babies occupied, busy, involved, and entertained. When browsing through a toy store, you can find different shapes, colors, and sizes of wind-up toys, busy boxes that make noise, and talking computers with colored graphics. While babies need stimulation, the question is what kind of stimulation is beneficial to babies' growth and development.

SCENARIO

A director was talking to a caregiver who believed that a two-month-old baby really loved watching her musical mobile that had green fish circling around and around. When the director asked the caregiver how she knew the baby loved the mobile, the caregiver said, "Because she stares and stares at it." Maybe this caregiver did not realize that moving objects mesmerize babies and shut down the thinking part of the brain. They see wind-up busy mobiles as entertainment objects for babies to begin to relate with. However, do young babies need a lot of complex busy objects?

What do infants need as first play objects? Actually, very young babies only need their own body. Babies come into this world equipped to play. Hands are babies' first play objects. They move them, gaze at them, suck on them, try to grasp with them; they float them through the air. You may not notice how babies use their hands. You may feel a need to put objects like rattles in babies' hands for them to be entertained or to develop concentration. This can interrupt the natural opportunity for babies to explore, experiment, and discover with their own hands. As babies develop their hand movement and coordination, they begin to grasp objects on their own. If toys and objects are within their reach, babies can decide when and what objects to manipulate and play.

What properties are important when selecting objects for babies? Consider the following guidelines when selecting toys and objects:

- ◆ Select objects that are safe and sturdy.
- ◆ Select objects that are simple.
- ◆ Select objects that are washable.
- ◆ Provide objects that are varied in size, shape, color, and texture.
- ◆ Provide objects that allow babies to make choices.
- ◆ Provide two to three objects per baby playing (not too many and not too few).
- ◆ Select objects that can be manipulated by the babies without adult intervention.
- ◆ Select objects that require no or little adult supervision.
- ◆ Provide objects that have different functions—a ball bounces, a rattle makes noise, and a car rolls—and objects that have multiple uses—a juice lid can reflect the light, make a noise when tapped on the floor, and feel smooth in the baby's hand.

◆ Safe and Sturdy

How safe do objects need to be? Safe enough for babies to put the objects in their mouths without swallowing the entire object or pieces of the object. Babies explore everything with their mouths. Sucking, licking, and tasting are their favorite ways to discover and relate to objects. When choosing objects, first make sure the object cannot go down the baby's throat.

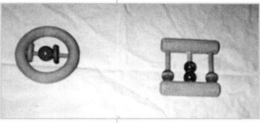

Examples of simple, safe, and varied play objects for babies.

An infant caregiver brought a small shiny pot to the infant room, explaining that the babies might be drawn to its reflective quality and the noise it made when banged. Although she was correct and it became a favored object for the babies, Marnie, a seasoned caregiver, became worried about the length of the handle on the pot. She voiced her concern, saying it made her anxious because she felt the babies could hurt themselves with the handle. The other caregiver honored Marnie's observations and removed the pot. It's very important to include the experiences and observations about safety of objects and equipment from the caregivers who work in the rooms. Caregivers have great observations about safety in infant rooms.

SCENARIO

◆ Simple

For very young infants, the objects should be simple and stay in place when put down. For example, a wooden rattle stays where it is placed as opposed to a ball that moves. Introduce the simplest objects at first. Simple and basic objects for infant play are soft dolls (eyes and nose sewn with thread) that have no small parts, cotton scarves (not silk because it can suffocate infants), teething rings, juice-lid tops with smooth edges, soft plastic hair rollers, rattles that show how the noise is made, small plastic cups or bowls. The idea here is that the object is passive and becomes active when the baby interacts with it. Active babies manipulate passive objects.

◆ Washable

All items that babies manipulate need to be able to be washed and disinfected. Stay away from dolls and stuffed animals that are filled with beaded material. Make sure dolls have sewn eyes and mouths. Wooden rattles can be soaked in mineral oil and or wiped with mineral oil or a cooking oil such as olive oil so they do not crack or split from washing with water. Provide enough objects to rotate throughout the day. Air dry objects by placing them in mesh bags. There are several environmentally friendly disinfectants available on the market. Some state regulations require using the standard bleach-and-water solution (one capful to one gallon of water) for cleaning and disinfecting toys. Always follow your state's guidelines for disinfecting toys and objects.

◆ Varied in Size, Color, Shape, and Texture

Offer babies objects in a variety of shapes and textures.

As infants develop, they will focus their explorations and develop their individual interests and preferences. To accommodate these explorations, provide objects with a variety of colors, and different sizes and shapes, such as a round ball and rectangular plastic boxes. Also include objects with different textures such as those that are soft, hard, smooth, and rough.

You can select two objects that are the same, but also offer a variety of objects for infants to explore differences. For older, more mobile infants, including some objects that move is important. Movements may interest the baby, such as a ball bouncing or a car rolling. Also, older infants like to gather and collect similar objects, such as several cups, bowls, or blocks, so make these objects available for their play.

◆ Allow Choices

A great way to provide opportunities for babies to make choices is with play. As babies manipulate and grasp the objects they choose, they figure out what they can do with the objects. Letting babies experience how they would play with toys is a great discovery process for them. The way you would play with a toy might be different than the way a baby plays with the toy. The best use of your time is to prepare the babies' environment so there are enough appropriate objects in a variety that meet the babies' interests and stages of development.

This baby looks quite interested in the multi-colored rattle.

◆ Not too Many and Not too Few Objects

You may think that providing more objects is better for babies so they have more objects from which to choose. However, babies may find it difficult to select an object when there are too many in front of them. Putting too much in the play area for infants can be overwhelming and overstimulating. This may cause babies to become irritable and cranky. One rule of thumb is to provide two or three objects per infant in the area and to limit the number of babies in the play space at a given time. Four or five babies playing near each other would need 8–12 objects in the environment. Too few objects may limit the baby's interest, choice, and discovery process. Monitor the play area throughout the day to keep a balance of simple and varied objects available to the babies in the play area. Clean and rotate the toys periodically, and select a few new ones to place in the play area. Leaving a few familiar objects in the play area shows that you are sensitive to the babies' need to stay orientated in their environment. This simple action demonstrates your awareness of the needs of the babies.

Provide just enough play objects for babies to explore.

◆ Can Be Manipulated by Babies Without Adult Intervention

Select objects that babies can interact with safely without an adult to show them "how" to use the toys. If a baby needs the assistance of an adult to interact with a toy or object, the object may be too complex for his or her stage. A toy that is too complex may stifle the baby's creativity and sense of self. Your main job is to observe the baby, to monitor his or her physical and emotional comfort, and determine if the baby has other needs. Babies know how to play. They don't need lessons. It is better to use your time to watch and enjoy how each baby plays in his or her environment.

◆ Different Functions

The best play objects are those that offer multiple uses and purposes. For example, balls bounce and roll, juice lid toys reflect, scarves change form, plastic cups bang, small metal balls clang, and so on. Infants learn about differences by exploring the many different things each object can do. Offer babies objects that can be used in different ways.

◆ Orderly Environments

Baby play spaces need to reflect a sense of order.

Babies are sensitive to order. They can experience physical and mental fatigue in a chaotic room. In the classroom, there should be a place for everything and everything in its place. This enables babies to learn from the very beginning that there is a sense of order to their surroundings. In an orderly environment, babies can see an object clearly, which helps their ability to concentrate.

To create and maintain a playroom that reflects order, consider the following guidelines:

- ◆ Prevent clutter.
- ◆ Check objects frequently for sign of wear and tear.
- ◆ Replace broken toys.
- ◆ Provide objects that have a variety of functions.
- ◆ Provide objects that infants can grasp on their own.
- ◆ Disinfect and prepare the play area before infants come to the playroom.
- ◆ Select toys and place them in various parts of the room.
- ◆ Rotate objects two to three times a day (always keep a few familiar objects in place).
- ◆ Watch and learn how babies use different objects (this will help you refrain from "teaching" the infant how to use an object).
- ◆ Allow infants to show interest in one another (infant-infant interaction is a great way for babies to socialize).

Prepare and monitor the babies' play space. There is a lot to consider to keep the space ready for the infants to explore. To select various appropriate objects and toys for the babies, you must think about which toys are best given the number of infants in your group and their developmental needs. Observing the babies as they play will help you determine what works and what doesn't. The babies will tell you what works when they play or don't play with certain objects. They will help you decide what to keep in or take out of the play environment.

Key Point

Babies can entertain themselves if they have a variety of simple basic objects that they can relate to and actively play with. Being entertained by overstimulating objects can influence babies to observe and become passive rather than active participants. You need to observe the actions of infants to develop and maintain interesting play environments with varied objects that allow babies to choose objects of interest to them. Showing babies how to use a toy can rob them of developing valuable creative problem-solving skills.

Solutions

- Develop play environments that are safe and offer a variety of basic objects that each have multiple functions.
- Allow babies to choose objects that interest them without much adult intervention and demonstration.
- Reduce chaos and overstimulation in babies' play spaces.
- Observe babies' exploration and play as ways to determine the appropriateness of play objects and babies' needs.
- Help families select toys that promote their baby's active participation.

Babies entertain themselves and show interest in simple, basic objects.

Chapter 28

The Room Environment: The Place and The Space

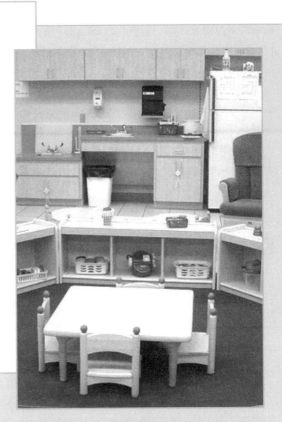

Issue

Developing a philosophy of care is crucial to the success of designing and setting up infant-care spaces. Many infant environments are set up in pre-existing spaces that may present challenges. Often caregivers are not consulted beforehand to provide feedback about the most efficient and appropriate way to set up and manage space. They may not been given opportunities to select furniture and equipment for their infant rooms. Caregiving is more efficient when there are designated areas for specific routines that are separate from play areas. Many infant areas do not reflect some of the basic components of safety, simplicity, and organization.

Rationale

Infant environments need to reflect efficient and effective organization of space for caregiving routines and babies' play exploration. Each area needs to have all the necessary equipment to carry out its specific function. Defining caregiving areas so they are separate from play spaces allows the caregiver and baby to stay focused on what they are doing. Play spaces need to be safe and stage-appropriate for free movement and exploration. Including staff recommendations and insights is beneficial in designing infant space.

Develop an inviting play space for babies to explore.

Goals

◆ To design and set up an environment for infants that reflects the philosophy of infant care

◆ To design efficient, effective, safe, and simple appropriate areas that are based on each area's function

◆ To separate caregiving spaces from high-traffic and designated play spaces

◆ To design space that reflects safe, simple, comfortable, and developmentally appropriate spaces for babies and caregivers

◆ To provide appropriate equipment in designated spaces

◆ To encourage feedback from infant staff about the effectiveness of the classroom space

Infant-care environments need to be functional and efficient for the caregivers and for the babies in the room. However, there may be certain obstacles that present a challenge in accomplishing this task. Given the opportunity, most infant caregivers would redo part of their workspace. Infant environments need to be designed to function efficiently and effectively. The areas in the room need to be child friendly as well as address the needs of the caregivers. In center-based care, most infant rooms are not built to the specific needs of babies. Infant rooms are often located in space that is not utilized for the older children in the center. When buildings are not specifically designed for infant-care spaces, caregivers and babies may find themselves in a space too large or too small, and the space may be one large room with no dividers. When caregivers are hired to work with babies, the classroom space and equipment are usually in place. Caregivers often have to make due with the existing cribs, changing tables, and other baby equipment. Rooms may be stark and uninteresting with very little variation of color and texture, or have equipment, patterns, and colors that are overstimulating for babies. For all these reasons, many caregivers who work with babies may need help designing the present space to be more functional and efficient.

Infant environments need to be designed to function efficiently and effectively.

An infant consultant visiting a new program noticed that the room was very sparse. She observed three infants playing with an empty cardboard box in one corner of the room. It was one of the only objects available to them. The room needed a fresh coat of paint and the floors needed to be cleaned. The room had plenty of natural light from several low windows. There was a second room that was used for storage that would have been perfect for a sleeping area. Just thinking about the possibilities energized the consultant, who helped the infant staff organize and utilize the space in the center. The caregivers welcomed the consultant's help in understanding which objects and furniture were appropriate to place in the room. Once the caregivers, with the consultant's help, designated the separate areas for physical care and play, they decided what equipment was needed in each of the areas. Most of the equipment was available in the storage room. Adding curtains and a few rugs softened the space and added an inviting look for both for the babies and staff.

SCENARIO

Infant rooms can be so stimulating that it feels overwhelming. The walls of the rooms are cluttered, and there is color bursting everywhere. Contraptions like swings and bouncy seats take up floor space, leaving little room for babies to move freely.

Organizing space for babies can be fun, but it takes thoughtful preparation. You will need to sketch and map where certain functional areas will be, such as diapering, eating, and playing. Write down a list of equipment. Draw on your map a picture of where the items should be placed. Your sketch needs to reflect how you interact with babies and what you believe and expect to happen throughout the day. For example, if you value babies' play and want a space for them to move freely, then your room design should reflect adequate space for babies based on their ability to explore. In addition, the space needs to represent efficient and functional areas. What do you do each day with the babies? Where do you do each activity or routine? Which spaces need to be near each other, and which ones should be separate from one another? Generally, space is limited by the mind of the designer. Another consideration is how many babies will be in the room. How many adults? What will these babies be able to do? Can they sit up, walk? Do you want walking babies with nonwalking babies? How long will the babies be in this room? These are a few of the issues needing to be discussed before setting up your environment so it meets the developmental stages of the babies in your care.

During a recent consultation for a new infant facility, the infant supervisor in charge of setting up the program was totally immersed in catalogs, selecting equipment for the infant environment. The consultant who was helping the infant supervisor was concerned that the infant supervisor would select purchases that were unnecessary and overlook equipment that could be useful. By talking with the supervisor, the consultant helped her design the space based on specific functions. They walked the room together, measured the space for specific needs and functions, and asked the staff for feedback before returning to the catalogs. These small measures helped create a more appropriate and functional space for both the babies and caregivers.

In designing infant room spaces, the most important consideration is to make the room safe for all the babies who will be in the room. It's important to go into the room, sit on the floor, and look around. From this vantage point, you will see what the baby will see. Lie on your back, look up, and then look sideways. Roll on your tummy and lift your head. Have you seen the baby's world through his or her eyes yet?

Consider the elements outlined on the following page when setting up an infant environment. The first group is important; the rest are optional, but would be valuable assets in infant rooms.

In designing infant room spaces, the most important consideration is to make the room safe for all the babies who will be in the room.

◆ Essential elements

The space must:
- ◆ Be safe for each baby
- ◆ Be functional, based on caregiving routines
- ◆ Have an available water source
- ◆ Have separate areas for eating, diapering, sleeping, and play, including quiet areas separate from active areas (quiet nook)
- ◆ Be easy to clean and disinfect
- ◆ Contain child-friendly furniture scaled to the size of the babies who are in the room (shelves, tables, and so on)
- ◆ Have equipment that supports infant caregiving (for example, eating area needs: chair, refrigerator, heating element for bottle, weaning table and stool, bibs, linen hamper, and so on)
- ◆ Be comfortable for adults to function during caregiving routines
- ◆ Contain storage for babies' food and personal items, and storage for adult personal items

An infant room should have clearly defined areas, child-friendly furniture, and comfortable furniture for caregivers.

◆ Optional but valuable elements

It would be ideal for the space to:
- ◆ Have natural light and proper ventilation
- ◆ have fresh air, with possible access to porch or deck for babies to move in and outdoors
- ◆ Have a quiet space for one or two babies to move away from group.
- ◆ have space for varied gatherings (for example, for reading a story; crawling up a play structure)
- ◆ Be inviting and pleasing to the eye
- ◆ Have soft textures (for example, a fringed rug, curtains)
- ◆ Have live nontoxic plants
- ◆ Have pictures at baby's level of real and familiar objects (for example, a baby, bird, ball)
- ◆ Have a play space away from caregiving activities (with wood floor if possible)
- ◆ Have a washer and dryer
- ◆ Have equipment for music (for example, tape recorder)

The room design needs to reflect what you do with babies throughout the day. For most of the day babies eat, sleep, get diapered, and play, so the room needs designated and separate space for each of those activities.

◆ Feeding Area

The feeding area needs to be away from high-traffic areas so it can offer a peaceful eating experience.

The feeding area is an active place and should be large enough to support at least two nonrocking chairs that are sturdy and have arms. Caregivers feed babies throughout the day. If there are three caregivers in the infant room, it is not uncommon for two babies and two adults to be in the feeding area at one time. The feeding area needs to be away from the play area, but it can be near the changing area. There needs to be a water source readily available and counter space for feeding equipment and storage. The feeding area needs to be away from high-traffic areas so that a one-on-one uninterrupted experience can occur between the caregiver and baby.

Suggested feeding equipment (see Chapter 23 for a more complete list of items):

- ◆ Two adult chairs for bottle and lap feedings
- ◆ Refrigerator
- ◆ Crock pot (out of the reach of infants) to heat bottles
- ◆ Adult chair for lap feeding
- ◆ Shelf for individual baby food and storage of feeding equipment
- ◆ Spoons, clear bowls, clear unbreakable glasses (small 1 oz.), bibs, washcloths, trays, hamper, garbage pail
- ◆ Weaning table and stool
- ◆ Sink with running water
- ◆ Flooring that is easy to clean, such as linoleum
- ◆ Available space for mothers to breast feed (privacy, adult chair, table)

Here is an example of equipment needed in a feeding area.

◆ Diapering Area

The diaper area requires a separate water source for hand washing. The diaper and feeding areas can be fairly close as long as you follow state regulations. Diapering is a special one-on-one time between you and the baby. The area needs to be away from high traffic patterns with no objects, mobiles, toys, or mirrors to distract from the relationship in diapering.

Diaper equipment (see Chapter 22 for a more complete list of items):
◆ Changing table
◆ Water source (sink with running water)
◆ Shelf with baby's individual supply of diapers, wipes, personal items
◆ Place for gloves, plastic bag, ointments
◆ Paper towels and/or washcloths
◆ Lidded diaper can
◆ Regular trash can
◆ Disinfectant

◆ Sleep Area

The sleep area needs to be in a quiet place away from other functions and activities. If the space is available and number of staff permits, having a separate sleep room is ideal. Often infant rooms are one large room that needs to be sectioned into several areas based on function. Using room dividers, bookshelves, drawer units, and other large equipment can be used to create separate spaces within one room.

Sleep equipment (see Chapter 24 for a complete list):
◆ Crib with futon, mattress, or mat, depending on your preference and state regulations
◆ Sheets and personal blankets (pastel colors preferably)
◆ Adult chair with rug on floor (optional)
◆ Small table lamp or night light nearby

◆ Play Area

The play space for infants needs to be away from physical care routines and sleep space. The area should have access to natural light, fresh air, and outdoor space, such as a porch, deck, or patio, if possible. Wood flooring is preferred for ease of babies' movement.

Babies can play comfortably when there is adequate space and equipment.

The play space should be large enough to allow for a physical structure, when appropriate. For young babies, a firm cushion is a good piece of gross motor structure. For older infants, the equipment could be a low wood platform or a wood structure with a few stairs to go up and down. Play spaces need to support play for an individual baby, two babies, or a small group of mobile babies, leaving enough space in the room for babies to move around and explore unhampered. The play space also needs to have a caregiver who is available to monitor babies' specific needs.

Play spaces often have a lot of traffic. Because babies play a lot, caregivers go to the play area to pick up or put down a baby several times during the day. It's important to be aware of the noise level in the play area and its effect on the babies. When two adults are monitoring the play space, they need to minimize talking and socializing when it doesn't involve the babies.

Play-area equipment (see Chapter 28 for a complete list):

◆ Large-motor structure, appropriate for the babies who are in the room
◆ structure for balance or small stair structure for mobile babies who are sitting up and creeping and crawling
◆ Low shelf secured to the wall
◆ Wood floor (preferred)
◆ Mobiles that represent things that fly in the air
◆ Nontoxic plants
◆ Rugs, curtains, floor mat
◆ Safety gate
◆ Books, tape recorder for music
◆ Soft area with mattress or child-size beanbag chair
◆ Variety of large manipulatives and small manipulatives
◆ Storage for toys (no lidded toy chests)
◆ Soft blocks
◆ Musical instruments and musical toys (for example, small piano, xylophone)
◆ Objects that roll (for example, balls, cars, trucks)
◆ Dolls; soft, stuffed teddy bears
◆ Plastic or wooden farm animals

(See the floor plan example on Appendix page 190–191.)

Designing infant space depends on many factors:

◆ Your philosophy of caring for infants
◆ The ability to separate care routines and play spaces
◆ Designing space based on caregiving needs
◆ The type and amount of space available
◆ The availability of a water source and its location
◆ The number of rooms available
◆ The creativity of the adults who design the space
◆ The developmental age and stage of the babies who will be in the room

Get feedback from caregivers about how the babies relate to each other and to the caregivers, and how the staff feels about the room, before adjusting or making changes. There's probably a designer and creator in every caregiver. Start today by asking yourself, "How well do I function in this room when I care for babies? What is one thing that I could improve in this room?" As babies grow and develop, you may need to change the space to accommodate their developing needs, especially their movement needs.

Babies need an environment that is not only pleasing and inviting but also efficient and effective for you and the babies in your care.

Remember, the environment that you and the babies use every day is an important ingredient in the success of daily routines with the babies. Babies need an environment that is not only pleasing and inviting but also efficient and effective for you and the babies in your care.

Key Point

Environments for infants need to have specific areas for caregiving practices that are separate from infant play spaces. Several basic and key elements need to be considered when designating appropriate and safe spaces for babies and caregivers to use competently and comfortably. Involving your coworkers as part of the brainstorming to develop the space in which they work will provide feedback that can lead to a more economic, efficient, and effective use of space.

Solutions

- Draw a sketch of designated spaces that reflects your philosophy of infant care.
- Provide safe environments for babies; this is crucial when setting up environments for them.
- Design space for specific care activities (for example, sleeping, feeding, diapering) with all necessary furniture and equipment.
- Separate care spaces from play spaces.
- Provide ample safe play space for different developmental stages of babies that allow movement and exploration.
- Provide access to outdoors.

Chapter 29

Watch Those Interruptions!

Issue

In order to thrive, babies need a peaceful environment where focused and attentive care is a priority. Interruptions fragment the caregiving relationship, disturb the atmosphere in the room, and add chaos.

Rationale

Decreasing and monitoring unnecessary interruptions in the environment helps you to say focused with the baby. Having clearly defined policies will help minimize chaos. These measures insure a more peaceful environment for you and the baby to enjoy and learn.

Goals

◆ To observe and determine how to minimize interruptions in your environment
◆ To have a clear understanding of your role as caregiver in relation to the caregiving process between you and the baby
◆ To be able to clarify your role to others
◆ To inform visitors about policies that relate to minimizing distractions when entering infant environments

As a caregiver in the infant room of a center-based facility, you are likely to experience many interruptions throughout the day: parents coming in and out, telephones ringing, staff wanting to talk about their latest problem, as well as your supervisor asking for information about what is happening in the room. Numerous interruptions can result in babies who are overstimulated and caregivers who are frustrated and frazzled. So how do you keep your frustration level down and your sanity intact?

Unfortunately, interruptions are a part of center-based care. Some interruptions are unavoidable and are a part of the day. For instance, when parents bring their infants into the center, in addition to wanting to connect with the caregiver about their baby, they may also want to talk about topics unrelated to the care of their baby. Another source of interruptions is other staff members who want to discuss issues other than those related to the care of the babies in the center. These discussions interrupt the continuity of care, which can lead to fragmented caregiving. When adults compromise the care process, the message to the baby is that he or she is less valued and respected as an individual. In addition, repeated interruptions disturb the atmosphere in the room, causing confusion and chaos, which does not contribute to a good learning environment.

SCENARIO

Margaret, the supervisor of an infant care center, received a message from Julia's mom stating Julia needed to be picked up for a doctor's appointment in less than one hour. Margaret quickly rushed into the infant room unaware of the activity and noise level currently in the room. Two mothers were standing in the middle of the room actively engaged in conversations and a father was holding his daughter, trying to settle her because she was crying. One caregiver was listening to an upset mom telling her about her baby's sleepless night. The other caregiver was bottle feeding a baby quietly in the corner of the feeding area. Margaret said to this caregiver, "Julia's mom is picking her up within the hour so be sure she has a fresh diaper." As the caregiver looked up and said, "What time is she coming?" she automatically stopped feeding the baby who began to cry loudly in protest. Margaret chose a caregiver based on whom she felt was the easiest to interrupt. She may have chosen the caregiver feeding the baby because it was a less stressful situation and the interaction was between the adult and baby instead of two adults.

In the scenario, Margaret's behavior and agenda got in the way of respectful caregiving, adding confusion by interrupting the caregiver who was feeding the baby. This created more chaos in the room and disrupted the feeding care process between the caregiver and baby. When adult agendas take priority over the needs of babies, this tells the babies that they are less important than the agenda.

If Margaret was more sensitive to what was happening in the infant room, when she entered the room she would have noticed the loud noise level. If she looked around, she would have seen several things happening that added to the chaos in the room—two mothers talking in the center of the room, a dad trying to quiet his upset baby, and a caregiver listening to a mom talk about her sleepless night with her baby. Margaret also would have noted a caregiver quietly feeding a baby his bottle in the corner of the feeding room. If Margaret was sensitive to providing attentive care to babies, she would have quietly asked the mothers in the room to carry on their conversation outside the room. She would have written a note about Julia's mom picking her up early and waited until the caregiver who was listening to the mother looked over at her. Then she would have gestured to the caregiver about the note before quietly leaving the room.

If Margaret was more aware of and sensitive to what was happening in the infant room, she might have chosen the least amount of interruption to deliver her message, as described in the revised scenario. Helping the two moms who were talking together in the center of the room to move out of the room gives them a gentle message about what is important for the babies and the caregivers. Margaret's sensitive choices in the revised scenario reflect the important message that she is aware of the effect of her behavior in relation to disruptions.

Ask adults not to interrupt when they see a caregiver engaged in caring for a baby.

Well-meaning caregivers can be the cause of interruptions. In one center, a consultant working to bring sensitive and responsive care into an infant program was concerned about the daily interruptions. She spent a day observing and making notes of the number and type of interruptions that interfered in the caregiving relationship. Later, the consultant discussed these findings with the supervisors and suggested strategies that could offset these distractions. One of the supervisors raised her concern that staff often talk about unrelated issues while caring for infants. A plan was discussed with the supervisors about what they would do to solve the issue. The following week, as the consultant was observing in the infant room, she noted that many of the solutions the supervisors came up with at the meeting were already in place, such as the following:

◆ Talking with infant-care staff about interruptions and the message they give
◆ Asking family members to be more sensitive when entering the infant room (post guidelines)
◆ Asking adults not to interrupt when they see a caregiver engaged in care
◆ Limiting siblings from going through the infant room (provide a place for them to wait)

These solutions decreased the number of unnecessary interruptions. As the consultant continued to watch the peaceful caregiving going on, two supervisors walked into the middle of the infant room and began discussing an administrative problem. As their discussion continued, they involved the caregiving staff by asking them questions. As a result, the infant staff became less involved in caregiving, and no one was watching or observing any of the babies.

All meaningful caregiving had stopped. No one was emotionally tuned in to what was happening with the babies. And, neither supervisor was aware that they had broken their own rules, interrupting the caregiving process. As role models for staff members, supervisors need to be aware that their behaviors reflect what they are asking of the staff. It's hard for supervisors to ask staff members to remain respectful and sensitive to the babies when the supervisors forget to model that philosophy in their own behavior. The important thing to remember is to continue support caregiving by decreasing the amount of interruptions.

Many factors affect the care process when there are frequent interruptions. Interruptions cause chaos, resulting in babies who are overstimulated and feel less valued. Also, it's hard to stay connected with babies when there is a lot of chaos or too much stimulation. Babies may tire more easily and get irritable when their senses are overloaded by too much happening in the room at one time.

Are you adding to unnecessary interruptions and to chaotic moments? If you believe that the needs of babies are important, it is easier to act more sensitively and model behaviors that influence others who are with babies.

Controlling the amount of interruptions will influence the caregiving process in a positive way. When other adults interrupt your time with the baby, gently look the adult in the eye and with a smile softly say, "I am with Dylan now. I will talk with you when I'm through." This is a gentle way to help others understand and experience what you believe. Hopefully, other adults will observe and learn from your modeling. Babies learn and thrive in peaceful environments that have few interruptions. To diminish interruptions, decrease:

Reduce interruptions by making the commitment that a baby comes first.

◆ Ringing telephones and phone messages,
◆ Idle and casual conversations between caregivers,
◆ Unnecessary caregiver-parent conversations,
◆ Staff-to-staff communications that are not about the babies, and
◆ The times when you play the radio, keeping it appropriate to the stage of the babies (not for more than 10–15 minutes).

Many interruptions between caregivers and babies happen throughout the day. Think about how much of your day is spent contributing to these interruptions. What could you do to minimize those times? If you decrease unnecessary interactions with other adults, what effect would it have on the babies and their environment? Maybe caregiving would become more meaningful and more peaceful. Remember, if you are not part of the solution in controlling interruptions, you are part of the problem. You can be sensitive and aware, and reduce interruptions by:

◆ Believing that each baby deserves to be valued and respected,
◆ Making a commitment that the baby comes first,
◆ Role modeling your belief by showing sensitive caregiving,

- Talking with coworkers about the things that interrupt caregiving processes and interactions in your room,
- Observing infants and watching how they learn from the adults and the environment around them, and
- Telling babies what you are going to do to stay focused while relating to the baby.

These suggestions are just a few. Can you think of one thing that will help you or your coworkers spend more uninterrupted quality time while you are involved in caregiving? Providing a small amount of uninterrupted time adds to the quality of your relationship with the babies in your care.

Key Point

Interruptions can be frequent in center care and affect the quality of the care process as well as add confusion and chaos in the room. How you value babies will affect the amount of interruptions you allow. Minimizing interruptions allows care to remain focused on babies and environments to be peaceful.

Solutions

- Believe that babies are valued individuals.
- Monitor interruptions with friendly reminders when needed.
- Model uninterrupted, focused care with babies.
- Design the environment to decrease chaos by planning efficient and effective space.

Chapter 30

Reflect Instead of Praise

Issue

Caregivers praise babies to let babies know that they value what the babies are doing. However, praising is also a judgment that tells the baby that you approve of them or their actions. While the goal of praise is to encourage the baby, the baby also learns to "perform for praise" and to rely on adult approval.

Rationale

Caregivers need to refrain from comments that praise and, therefore, judge babies' actions. These judgments may affect a baby's motivation to do things for himself or herself. Responding to babies by using reflective language reinforces babies' feeling of self-worth. This allows babies to act for their own pleasure and sense of accomplishment.

Goals

◆ To understand that praise is judgmental
◆ To understand the difference between praise and reflection
◆ To reinforce reflective responses by adults

"Good job." "Good boy." "Great girl." "That makes me happy." These comments send powerful messages to babies throughout their day that are meant to reinforce babies' self-esteem. Because praise is given so often, it is worth taking a look at what praise is all about and its possible consequences. To praise means to admire, to give tribute, or to award. In addition, the underlying message of praise is "I approve or disapprove," which is what babies learn to accept. This teaches babies to seek out adults for acceptance, for a measure of their self-worth. But you may say, "What is wrong with this? I've been praising children for years" or "This is how I was raised" or "My mother praised me, and I turned out okay."

Consider how praise affects self-confidence and motivation. Confidence comes from within; it is the knowledge that you can do something. Relying on comments by others to know what you can or can't do will make you vulnerable. It is impossible for someone to always be there to comment on your behavior. It is far better for a baby to learn something because she wants to learn it, to satisfy her own drive, ambition, and desires. The motivation to do well or to try to do something new needs to be self-directed and self-motivated.

Repeated praise and approval by adults leaves a baby vulnerable to relying on adult responses for validation. Praise can also develop egos that are fragile—the baby's motivation and confidence is affected when adults approve or disapprove their actions.

What you do when babies play is one example of how you judge babies. When you interfere with babies' play by trying to show babies how to play and or how to use a toy, you are offering praise and, therefore, judgment. You are judging babies when you approve of what they are doing by saying, "Good job" or clapping enthusiastically when they play. One caregiver said, "When I watch babies' play without interfering, I'm in awe at their ability and concentration. To see how they manipulate and twist a certain toy this way or that. Sometimes I think, 'How clever!' I wouldn't have thought to do it that way." This caregiver understood the value of what the baby was doing. She was able to quietly watch the baby without interrupting and judging the baby's actions. When you refrain from judging the actions of babies, it supports the babies' creativity and independence, and stops you from raising "praise junkies." The scene below is an example of how this happens.

Eight-month-old Beth climbs up the slide structure in the playroom. She reaches the top, and sits down with a sense of great satisfaction. Casey, the caregiver in the playroom, goes over to Beth smiling and clapping her hands saying, "Good job, Beth! Good job!"

> Confidence comes from within; it is the knowledge that you can do something.

SCENARIO

Is this kind of praise appropriate or unnecessary? Using praise teaches babies to act for adults rather than for their own pleasure. Constant praise affects the baby's motivation to act. Eliminating praise comments is difficult. What should you do instead to comment on baby's behaviors? The answer is acknowledgement and reflection.

◆ Acknowledge and Reflect

One way to acknowledge babies is to comment on your observations as you watch them. For example, in the scenario described above with Beth, who goes up the slide structure for the first time, Casey could have said, "Beth, I saw you go up the slide. You look pleased with yourself." Reflecting, or acting as a mirror, about what you see happening without judging or praising lets the baby know you noticed her effort and ability. Using this technique makes a difference in the life of young babies. They learn to appreciate their efforts without having to please someone else; they learn the pleasure of satisfying themselves.

Acknowledging and reflecting babies' efforts takes practice and a belief that praising negatively affects motivation and behaviors. Muriel, the caregiver to 13-month-old Keisha, has successfully learned to acknowledge Keisha without judging. When she saw Keisha complete a two-piece puzzle and look up at her, Muriel smiled stating, "I saw you put the puzzle together; you look very happy about putting the puzzle together." Muriel validated Keisha's behavior without judging her performance.

The chart below outlines a few examples of reflective responses verses responses.

Praise responses	can be replaced by	Reflective responses
Yeah! You grasped the ball.		I see you grasped the ball.
Good job! You climbed up the ramp.		I saw you climb up the ramp. You look pleased.
Good boy, you ate all that food!		Yes, you ate all your lunch.
Wow! Super, you stacked the cups!		I saw you stack the cups.
I love you when you hug me.		Thanks for the hug.

Reflective responses are meant to acknowledge what is going on or happening. "I see," "I hear," and "I notice" are simple beginnings for statements you can make. They eliminate praising and judgmental comments. Below are a few suggested behaviors that you can use to promote a reflective attitude.

◆ Practice reflecting on what you see happening.
◆ Spend time observing the baby.
◆ Appreciate what the baby can do.
◆ Slow down and eliminate your personal agenda.
◆ Avoid praising and passing judgment on behaviors.
◆ Respond to, rather than directing, what the baby is doing.
◆ Support the baby's actions and feelings when you observe them.

Practicing these behaviors will help to acknowledge rather than judge babies' efforts. When you reflect and acknowledge, you let babies know that you are interested. Babies learn that they are special and accepted for what they do in their own way.

Babies express delight when acknowledged as special in their own way.

Key Point

Caregivers need to acknowledge and reflect on babies' actions without judging them. Praising babies makes them dependent on approval from adults. This can make them motivated to please others instead of themselves.

Solutions

◆ Avoid praise comments directed to babies.
◆ Acknowledge babies efforts by reflecting on what you see.
◆ Replace praise responses with reflective responses.
◆ Refrain from value judgments.

Chapter 31

To Touch or Not To Touch: There Is No Question

Issue

Respectful touching is when you tune in to babies' needs and are aware of your motivations about when to touch babies. But, sometimes babies are touched needlessly. It is critical to distinguish between soothing and timely touches and touching that is undesirable and disruptive.

Rationale

Respectful touching of babies is essential for their well-being. Observing babies, announcing what you are going to do before doing it, and asking a baby's permission to touch shows that you are sensitive to them as individuals. Being sensitive to babies includes knowing when to touch and realizing that your touch can also interfere with a baby's desire and interest.

Goals

- ◆ To be sensitive to the needs of the baby regarding touch
- ◆ To understand that touch supports bonding and can be soothing
- ◆ To be aware that touch can disrupt and interfere with babies' desires and interests
- ◆ To ask permission before touching babies (reaching out or toward you with their arms or scooting/crawling to you indicates permission; behaviors that do not demonstrate permission are when a baby turns his or her whole body away, shuts his or her eyes, or turns his or her head away from you)

Touch provides a warm, safe haven.

To touch and to be touched is a basic human need. It is a powerful human connector that can reinforce a bond between humans, and it is a way of communicating. When touch is done at the right moment with permission, it can provide the soothing that is needed. However, touch is a very personal preference that needs the consent of the person being touch in order to be respectful. Though touch can be soothing, it can also be offensive when not desired. A potentially soothing touch can become an invasion of one's space or privacy.

What can you do in your group care situation to support respectful touching? First, check with your state regulations about policies concerning handling of babies. Then, you can ask permission from the baby: "Do you want me to hold you?" This simple request lets the baby know you are sensitive to what he or she might want. How many times have you witnessed enthusiastic adults touching babies without permission? Tousling their hair, pinching their cheeks, or jiggling their feet are a few things adults do with babies. These gestures give babies the message that they are objects to be dabbled with. The next time you witness this kind of act, watch the baby's body language. You might be surprised by what the baby shows you. Touching babies without telling them what you are about to do or without asking their permission reflects a belief that babies are unaware of what is happening and what you do with them makes little difference. This attitude disregards babies' individual feelings.

◆ Do Not Mess with Contentment

See how focused this baby is as he explores a toy.

When you see that babies are content, leave them be. When you touch babies who are busy, you give them the message that what they are doing is less important than what you want. You may have witnessed countless interruptions by well-meaning adults who decide to cuddle or hold a baby who is busy with his or her own activity.

Joshua and Hannah, both mobile infants, were playing near a window when a bird flew to the window and began eating from the birdfeeder. Both babies began to watch intently as the bird ate his seed. Nora, the caregiver, watching the babies in the playroom came to the scene and said gleefully, "Oh, look at the bird!" Nora picked Hannah up to look out the window. Both children were distracted by Nora's interruption as the bird flew away from the scene.

How long would Joshua and Hannah have had the pleasure of watching the bird if it hadn't been for Nora's interruption? This subtle scene happens often in care situations—a baby's concentration is interrupted from his or her peaceful interests. The caregiver may not recognize that their behavior disturbs the baby's interest.

When you touch, cuddle, and move babies for no good reason, your actions are telling the babies that what they are doing is less important than what you want. What message is given to babies when you choose to act on your needs above the babies'? Will they feel more or less important? What about their feelings? Will they be frustrated? Does this show the infants that they are valued?

◆ Observe Babies to Determine What They Need

Although babies need touch to thrive, it is essential to determine when touch is a help to the baby or a hindrance. Observing the baby is the key to the answer. Some babies may ask to be touched for reassurance or nurturance. For instance, when walking by, they reach out their hands to you to be picked up. Mobile infants move away from and come back to adults often for emotional "refueling." Tired and crying babies may need your support with a soothing touch. Babies who are tired or overstimulated need you to respond by taking them away from the group to a quieter part of the room environment, or if they are overtired, they may need to go to their bed for rest. It is important to observe and know when babies need you.

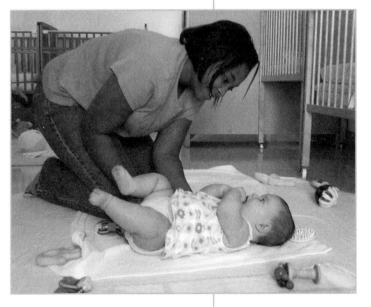

Observing the baby is the key to knowing when touch is a help or a hinderance.

To determine when and how to be available, look at the baby and try to understand his or her need. Remember to evaluate whose need is it to touch or be touched—yours or theirs? Look at the baby to get the answer.

<table>
<tr>
<td>

Key Point

</td>
<td>

Being aware of babies' needs and wishes is key to respectful touching. Asking permission from babies lets them know that you are sensitive to their wants and desires.

</td>
</tr>
</table>

Solutions

◆ Touch babies based on their wishes and needs.

◆ When babies are content, do not interfere with what they are doing.

◆ Ask yourself, "What message am I giving babies when I touch them?"

◆ Ask baby's permission to touch by simply saying, "May I pick you up?" or "Do you want me to hold you?"

Chapter 32

Quality Care

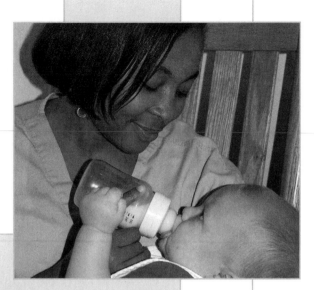

Issue

Many babies up to 15 months old are in group care a good part of their day. Every baby has the right to high standards of quality infant care. The basic elements of quality care help insure that babies and their families receive appropriate practices that promote infant develop and well-being. Although these standards have been well documented (Bredekamp & Copple, 1997; Gerber & Johnson, 1998; Zero to Three, 1995), some of these practices are not yet a part of infant-center care.

Rationale

High-quality care enriches the baby's daily experiences with caregivers while providing support to their families. Developmentally appropriate practices have been identified that provide babies with quality care in infant programs. These practices include the following:

◆ Primary care
◆ High staff-to-infant ratios
◆ Small group size continuity of care
◆ Responsive caregiving
◆ Meeting the individual needs of babies and their families
◆ Understanding cultural, linguistic, and family diversity
◆ Maintaining health and safety practices
◆ Providing a well-designed and well-managed environment
◆ Education and training of staff

When these practices are in place in infant programs, babies, families, and caregivers have a better chance to thrive.

Goals

◆ To define quality care
◆ To identify and explain the key factors in quality care
◆ To discuss ways of providing infants and families with quality care in center care

In a center, quality care means that infants and their families are involved in an ongoing, relationship-based care process with a primary caregiver who provides responsive care that is sensitive to the needs of infants and families placed in their care. Listed below are key factors that influence how quality care can be carried out in center care.

◆ Primary Care

Primary care is when a caregiver is "in" a special relationship with a small group of babies (three to four) where mutual trust and respect for one another develops over time. This person knows and understands the babies' cues, needs, and preferences and by relating together, the babies begin to know and trust the caregiver. This connection allows the babies to signal their caregiver in times of physical and/or emotional need. They are so in tune in their relationship that their communication together says, "I want to know and understand who you are, and I want you to know and understand me as well." Some benefits of primary caregiving are that it deepens the bonds of attachment, offers predictability, and creates a secure base for babies to explore their world (Lally, 1995). The caregiver is able to predict and manage behaviors and enjoy seeing their babies grow and develop (see pages 31–33 for more information on primary care).

◆ Staff-to-Infant Ratios

Recommended ratios of adult caregiver to infant is one adult to three or four infants (1:3 or 1:4), with the average of seven or eight babies per room space. When these recommendations are followed, babies have less cry time, are more cooperative, have more spontaneous verbalizations, and respond to interactions more frequently.

◆ Continuity of Care

Continuity of care means that caregivers stay with babies through a period of development from three to 18 months or three months to three years. Continuity also means maintaining staff that follow a philosophy that includes giving babies care from beginning to the end of care. This also means giving babies care by one primary person who carries out routines, such as diapering or eating, from the beginning of the task to the end without interruption or a break in the care process.

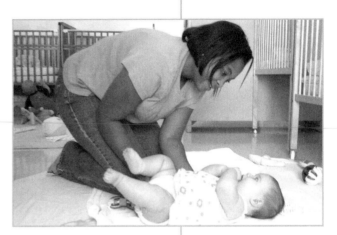

This baby and caregiver are enjoying their caregiving relationship.

◆ Responsive Caregiving

When caregivers are sensitive to and tuned in to the individual needs of the baby based on observations, the care is apt to be reciprocal and responsive. An example of a reciprocal experience between the caregiver and the baby is when 11-month-old Samual climbs on the stairs that are a part of the gross motor structure and, upon his descent, begins to cry in distress. The caregiver moves closer and says, "Samual, do you need some help getting down?" Samual reaches for the caregiver who reacts to him by saying, "Let me help you to get down the stairs." She reaches out her arms to Samual to assist him to move down the stairs.

◆ Meeting Individual Needs of Babies and Their Families

Babies have a sense of their own body rhythm and rely on caregivers to learn what their bodies are telling them. When the caregiver does this, the babies are reassured that what their bodies said is correct. This helps babies to understand what their bodies have told them is true and strengthens their trust in the caregivers. Family members are able to trust caregivers when they see a mutually satisfying and respectful relationship caregivers and babies have together.

◆ Understanding Cultural, Linguistic, and Family Diversity

Respecting values, cultural practices, and parenting styles of individual families allows open communication and avoids misinterpretations and misunderstandings between families and caregivers. When families feel valued for their cultural practices, they are more apt to be involved in a cooperative partnership with you. Adding books, pictures, music, and tapes that reflect diverse populations lets families know you are sensitive to them.

◆ Maintaining Health and Safety Procedures

When safety and health policies are in place for the common good of the center and community, all members are better protected. Following state guidelines and having a parent handbook with specific health and safety policies are important so all participants understand the policies.

◆ Providing a Developmentally Appropriate, Well-Designed, and Well-Managed Space

The environment for babies needs to be safe, to appeal to the senses, and to be appropriate for the stage of the babies. Ample storage is critical. Having access to indoor and outdoor space is ideal. Porches, decks, platforms, and yard surfaces add interest to infant spaces. Providing shade and different texture surfaces (grass, sand, wood) allows babies to explore a variety of surface areas. The average indoor space for five to six babies is about 350 square feet and for nine mobile infants is about 500. Babies need on average 25 feet per child for outdoor space (see Chapter 28 on environments for more details).

◆ Education and Training of Staff

Caregivers are the center's most valuable resource because they make a difference in the lives of the babies they care for and about. Providing training for individual caregiver needs as well as in-service training for all staff supports and re-energizes caregivers. Bringing in guest speakers and helping to finance professional conferences are a few options in providing professional development.

Key Point

Following quality care practices helps to promote the well-being of babies and families involved in group care. Creating a primary relationship based on mutual trust and understanding deepens the attachment between baby, caregiver, and family.

Solutions

- ◆ Enter into a special relationship with each baby in your care.
- ◆ Foster mutual trust and respect between you, the babies, and their families.
- ◆ Place babies in small groups based on compatible stages.
- ◆ Keep ratios of caregiver and babies low (one caregiver to no more than four babies to care for—1:4).
- ◆ Be sensitive to family values and cultural patterns.

Chapter 33

Working Together With Families

Issue

Providing quality care relies on open communication between caregivers and families about specific issues relating to their babies' well-being. Although caregivers can be a valuable resource to families and families can offer valuable information to caregivers about their babies, too often these alliances break down by unnecessary comments about personal problems, in-house issues, or gossip. Crossing professional lines (for example, babysitting for the family of a child in your group) is almost always detrimental to quality infant care.

Rationale

Building strong relationships and alliances between families and caregivers increases the possibility of providing quality care for babies. Families can provide valuable insights and information to help caregivers understand their baby. Often, families have important information about babies' habits that help caregivers interpret their needs. In addition, caregivers can support families and develop mutually trusting professional relationships with them.

Goals

◆ To foster communication that supports a professional alliance with families
◆ To utilize important information families offer about their babies
◆ To keep channels of communication open with families
◆ To choose times to discuss specific issues with families without jeopardizing responsibilities or compromising safety
◆ To refrain from discussing in-house problems or gossip with families

What you know about the babies in your care is an important source of information for families. Families often seek advice from caregivers, especially when it is their first baby. Today's families may not have the benefit of nearby relatives and may turn to you or their pediatrician for advice and support. A relationship with the baby's family forms early, and continues as you share in their delight as their baby reaches milestones. Your daily contact with their baby forms a bond that they begin to rely on and look forward to for valuable information. Providing families with information about their babies can lead to families providing valuable insights for you about their child. This sharing of information can deepen the bond between you and the families, which can ease some of their anxieties and increase their trust in you. When families see you incorporating their baby's preferences into your interactions with their baby, they feel valued and connected with you as someone they can rely on to care for their baby. Being sensitive and open to learning about the family's child-rearing practices and their family culture helps you understand different parenting styles.

SCENARIO

Mrs. Gonzales came with her baby to visit the center before Jose was to start full time. Sarah, the caregiver, gave Mrs. Gonzales information about how the infant room functions. She described what a normal day will be like for Jose while Mrs. Gonzales is at work. Sarah was careful to explain the center's philosophy of caregiving so that Mrs. Gonzales would understand why certain things are done. Sara also found time to show Mrs. Gonzales where all her baby's personal items would be stored. As the morning went by, 11-month-old Jose became very cranky and started to suck his two fingers as he began to cry. Mrs. Gonzales told Sarah, "Oh, that's his hungry cry. He always puts those two fingers in his mouth when he is hungry." Sarah noted this information about Jose's eating cue. She knew it would be helpful in knowing when to feed Jose. Later, as Mrs. Gonzales was observing the caregiving and babies in the room, Jose began to kick his arms and legs vigorously. Mrs. Gonzales said to Sarah, "May I use the changing table? Jose needs a diaper change." Sarah asked how Mrs. Gonzales knew that. She responded, "When I watched him kicking, I saw that his diaper was soiled."

Families offer valuable cues that can be very helpful to caregivers. Giving care that is similar to what the family gives helps the baby's adjustment to the center. When the baby knows that you understand what certain behaviors mean, the child experiences what is familiar to him.

Unproductive interactions with families can have damaging effects on the program as well as the babies in your care and their families. Avoid any of the following:

◆ Gossiping about another staff member with a family member
◆ Complaining about the administration or one of their decisions
◆ Discussing babysitting plans
◆ Talking about a difficult baby in your care
◆ Discussing your own personal problems
◆ Rehashing the terrible news of the day

Engaging in casual conversations with family members takes your focus and attention away from your job of caring for babies. This can endanger the safety of the babies and compromise their well-being. These conversations can also have a damaging effect on your program. Caregivers working with babies may need to talk to parents in the beginning and end of the day. These interactions are important in bonding and aligning with parents of babies in your care. However, these connections should be done without compromising the safety of the babies in your care, and the conversation should provide specific information about their baby. You need to continue to observe and monitor your room during these brief encounters to be certain that the babies are safe and satisfied. Some caregivers miss adult conversations and extend communication beyond safe limits. Be professional about what to say and when to talk to parents.

Families need to be a part of a partnership with you, the professional caregiver.

When you engage in overly familiar conversations with a family member, the professional relationship between you and the family is at risk. Being friendly but professional in your relationship with families creates clear boundaries and lets the families know that you view yourself as a professional who chooses to be with babies. This means you are serious about what you do and the care you provide to babies. When you maintain these clear boundaries, it will be easier for you to discuss specific issues and concerns about their baby.

Relationships with families are important and valuable to developing and maintaining quality service to young children who are in center-based care. Families need to be a part of a partnership with you, the professional caregiver. Keeping open communication between adults provides positive partnerships that aid the care of their baby. Alliances between you and families provide information that can be valuable to the baby's well-being. Both you and the children's families need to support and maintain this partnership in order for babies to thrive in center-based care.

As the front-line caregiver, you can choose to make a difference in your program. Hopefully, you believe you can make a favorable difference. Helping families understand how to spend time with their baby allows them to have pleasurable alone times needed for their own "refueling." A few helpful tools families can do at home that help them in determining when and how to spend time include the following:

◆ **Develop a safe, gated play space at home** where baby can move and explore his or her environment but see and hear everyone at home. This idea relieves family members from carrying the baby while doing other things.

◆ **Place babies on their backs on the floor for brief periods of time** early in the baby's life. Provide a blanket for babies to lie on with a few toys nearby and watch what their babies do. This is a wonderful way to enjoy the baby.

◆ **Model responsive physical care** (for example, diapering) so parents can observe how full attention, telling baby what is happening, and including baby in the care process provide rich experiences that meet the baby's social and emotional needs, so he or she is better able to play and explore on his or her own.

Adults who care for infants need to take care of themselves so that they can joyfully take care of babies. The same is true for you, the caregiver.

Key Point

Forming professional alliances between caregivers and their families offer families support that they may not receive from friends or relatives. It's important for the caregiver to provide communication that is useful and valuable to families about their babies. This needs to be done while maintaining a professional relationship. Families also provide valuable information to caregivers about their babies. Unproductive discussions can hurt important relationships. Communication needs to be given without jeopardizing the safety of the infants in your care.

Solutions

◆ Maintain a professional relationship with families.
◆ Promote alliances with families based on babies' behavior, progress, and needs.
◆ Keep lines of communication open and specific to parent-child issues, avoiding unnecessary in-house issues and gossip.
◆ Include valuable cues families offer about their baby in your daily care.

Chapter 34

Questions Frequently Asked By Families

Issue

During tours of a center, the most frequently asked questions by families are about caregivers. The answers to these questions help families understand what will happen with their baby and ease their anxiety. The responses also help them make informed decisions about their baby's placement.

Rationale

Families need to observe the infant center they are considering. The tour they receive will provide valuable information to help them make a decision about placement for their baby. One way families express their concerns and, maybe, their apprehension about placing their baby in group care is by asking questions. Answering families' questions and providing information can help ease their anxiety as they prepare to entrust their baby in the care of another person.

Goals

- ◆ To understand that information helps ease families' anxiety
- ◆ To respond to families' questions during and after the enrollment process
- ◆ To provide families with a tour of the faculty
- ◆ To inform families of safe and healthy infant-care practices

If the center you work in conducts tours for interested families who are considering placing their infant in your infant program, you may want to know questions that families frequently ask when visiting centers. Most frequently asked questions from families about center-based care are about the caregiving staff. Families wanted to know who would be with the infants. They wanted to know staff qualifications and length of employment. This reflects the importance in the first year of life of the relationship that forms between the infant and adult, and how it is vital and essential to the baby's health.

Listed below are the questions frequently asked:
1. What are the qualifications of the staff?
2. What are the ratios in the infant room, the number of babies and the number of staff?
3. Who will take care of my baby?
4. How long has this caregiver been employed at the center?
5. What type of schedule will the baby follow?
6. Do the caregivers have CPR and first-aid training?

By looking at these questions, it is obvious that the families are most concerned about who will be with their baby on a daily basis. The recent articles about how infants learn and absorb information in the first year of life have hit the newsstands. Families today understand the important role caregivers play in the development of their children and in supporting families in child-rearing practices.

Families have more knowledge about what to expect in a quality child-care center. They usually want to visit and observe the center they are considering. They come prepared with information, questions, and a pad and pencil. Although tours are a common practice today and an important part of any child care selection, they are more common today than in the past.

Families have a lot of concerns and anxieties about leaving their babies in someone else's care. Their questions need to be heard and answered. As infant caregivers, you should welcome and appreciate families' questions. Provide them with information so they can make informed decisions and ease their anxieties about placement.

Remember, when it comes to their babies, families may find it hard to relinquish their role as caregiver—even for short periods of time. Imagine what it might be like having your baby at home for two to three months and then returning to work? It cannot be easy to leave your baby in the arms of someone who is almost a perfect stranger. You want to know this person who will care for your baby. Parents have many mixed feelings about child-care centers and whether their baby will be cared for properly. In some ways, the anxiety families feel may be due to the emotional bond they have with their child.

Families have a lot of concerns and anxieties about leaving their babies in someone else's care. Their questions need to be heard and answered.

You can begin to develop the families' trust. Your sensitive understanding about how difficult it is for them to entrust their little ones in your care is a good beginning. A director of a large infant-toddler center confided that about one in 10 parents on her waiting list decided to quit work and stay at home. There is a tremendous bond between families and babies that influences their behaviors and decisions. When families decide to use center care, you can help them to define what is safe and reasonable to expect for their baby.

One very easy way to convey this message is to allow families to experience how serious your center is about the safety and well-being of the infants in your care. An infant center that is committed to quality has a small list of "must do's" upon entrance. "Please remove your shoes and wash your hands before entering the infant room" is at the top of the list. Right from the start the family gets the message that this is a special place where healthy practices are maintained for infant safety.

Families have apprehensions and anxieties in the initial phase of enrollment. Including families in the enrollment process is a must. You and the family need to begin to know, understand, and trust one another. This can best be done through personal contact, which is much more than being friendly. It's a contact that will eventually turn into a trusting alliance between you and the child's family. At one infant center, the caregiver visits the home and then the baby and a family member come in for a warming-in period several days before enrollment. It's time well spent. The caregiver finds out information about the family and the families are able to see first hand how babies are being cared for. One mother, who watched her four-month-old baby Kyle being fed, appreciated the caregiver asking if there was anything in particular she could do for Kyle differently during his bottle feeding. Later on the mother stated, "I really appreciated being asked if there was anything that needed to be done special for Kyle."

During times when you and the babies' families are together, it's important to ask a few questions about their particular baby's routine:
1. Tell me about your baby's eating habits.
2. How do you know when your baby is finished eating?
3. Does your baby enjoy eating most foods?
4. How do you hold your baby when he is drinking his bottle?
5. Do you do anything special during feeding that we might need to know?

These questions let families know you are interested in getting to know their baby and his or her routine. It also lets the families know you are sensitive to their baby's routines. This helps in forming trusting alliances between you and the families.

When families decide to use center care, you can help them to define what is safe and reasonable to expect for their baby.

Remember, families make decisions based on how they feel about their center visit. What they experience, and how well their questions are answered, impacts their decision for choosing placement. Your presence influences their decision and selection. As you respond to questions from families, keep in mind the following question: "Would I want to put my baby here?"

Key Point

Expect and welcome families' questions as they consider caregiving options for their baby. Give information and provide home visits and on-site tours to ease families' anxieties. Supporting communication with families and building alliances with them helps to develop trust. These alliances begin on first contact.

Solutions

◆ Respond to families' questions during the enrollment process.
◆ Support alliances with families for trust to develop between you and the families.
◆ Actively engage families during on-site tours.
◆ Provide information to ease families' anxieties.
◆ Ask for families' feedback about their baby's specific routines.

Chapter 35

Nurturing the Caregiver

Issue

Caring for babies is a demanding responsibility. To give babies the proper care, you need to take care of yourself. In so doing, you will maintain your health and avoid burnout.

Rationale

Work-related issues can undermine the satisfaction and joy you experience when caring for babies. Coping with these stressors is necessary to retain your emotional and physical well-being. There are many methods to use to avoid burnout.

Goals

◆ To maintain and care for yourself
◆ To identify signs of burnout
◆ To communicate positively
◆ To express and understand your feelings
◆ To discover personal strategies that refresh, replenish, and relax you

To be a caregiver means to care for someone without asking for anything in return. This is an enormous task. Some caregivers are good at meeting the needs of others but fall short in taking care of themselves. Some caregivers forget to refill their own "glass" and face burnout. If you are feeling burned out, it is easy to feel frustrated or become impatient. You may feel angry and taken advantage of. Are you feeling down in the dumps for no good reason? Have you been late or absent from work more than usual? Are you feeling unappreciated? All of these feelings may be symptoms of burnout.

The staff members and caregivers at a child-care center noticed that Amanda, who was usually a perceptive and friendly administrator of the center, was looking harried, hurried, and unhappy. When anyone approached her, she was snappy and short with her messages, often barking orders as she went out the door. Many noted that they often saw her frowning while mumbling under her breath.

These behaviors are typical of someone who is suffering from burnout. Amanda needs a change of pace—a break from her work routine. Her battery needs recharging. When you see and experience a coworker with burnout, it is not pleasant to watch or be a part of. Do not take your coworker's behavior personally; remind yourself that this person feels that his or her "cup is half empty." Suggest a lunch date or a walk in the park, or even a day off as a breath of fresh air. Letting the person know that you are concerned may help him or her take care of himself or herself and reduce burnout. Burnout leads to being miserable at work or even quitting.

Some caregivers are good at meeting the needs of others but fall short when taking care of themselves.

Taking care of yourself is essential in maintaining your career. It can be difficult to keep your cooperative spirit and positive attitude. Generally speaking, in the child care field, burnout is high, and benefits can be limited. Many centers have high children-to-adult staff ratios, which can put several babies in one group. Dealing with families, administrators, staff, and children can be taxing and overstimulating. Local, state, and federal laws often put constraints on child care centers, which can be overwhelming.

However, if you value working with young children, you tolerate these work conditions. As you persevere in your profession, it is important to find ways to maintain your health and well-being and prevent burnout. Some coping mechanisms to consider include keeping the channels of communication open and expressing your feelings in ways that can be heard.

◆ Open Communication

- ◆ Keep the channels of communication open with the babies, parents, administrator, coworkers at your center, and with other professionals in the field.
- ◆ Avoid accusations that make people defensive. State your issues in a positive way. For example, "Have you tried…?" "What do you think about…?" "Have you noticed…?"
- ◆ Avoid gossip; it is hurtful to all parties, including you, and can add to needless confusion.
- ◆ Observe what is happening; try not to assume what is happening. When in doubt, ask for more accurate facts or information.
- ◆ Reserve making judgments and being critical of situations or behaviors.

Taking care of yourself is as important as taking care of babies.

◆ Express Your Feelings

- ◆ Express your feelings in ways that can be heard. When you allow your feelings to collect and bottle up, they can lead to explosions.
- ◆ Try to identify what you are feeling. Explore your feelings and identify the origin of what is going on with you.
- ◆ When your emotions are in check, express your feelings to the appropriate person. Showing anger when you are trying to make a point with someone puts them on the defensive and dilutes your message. Often the receiver focuses on the intense emotion rather than the message you are trying to convey. Sometimes people withdraw during emotionally charged conversations. This may be a defense against losing control, becoming emotionally overwhelmed, or doing something or saying something they will regret later.

Delores was quite taken aback when Faith became angry at her for being 10 minutes late from her break. She listened to Faith's ranting and raving a few minutes before feeling overwhelmed and anxious. "Faith, I know you are angry at me for being late. I'll explain to you when I see you later after your break. Right now, I'm going out with the children." Often removing yourself from an emotionally charged situation can dilute the confrontation. It is essential to reconnect later with the person to reach an understanding and clear up any misconceptions.

Maybe you are the type of person who needs help to identify, clarify, and express your feelings. What then? Journaling is one way to keep in touch with how you feel about your day, noting the significant events and how you felt. Taking time to write down your thoughts will help you sort out feelings and understand specific patterns of behaviors. Journaling also develops skills that are useful in your daily observation and caregiving practice. Journaling makes you more aware of what you are doing, which can only help your practice.

When you tend to know how you feel, solutions to situations become simpler, clearer, and less intense. You could also try to find a mentor to talk to who will listen—a person who is knowledgeable and experienced in your field, a person you respect and trust for guidance and support. Sharing a cup of coffee with a friend and venting can offer a fresh view of the situation and allow a more realistic and manageable approach to surface. You might easily resolve your concerns.

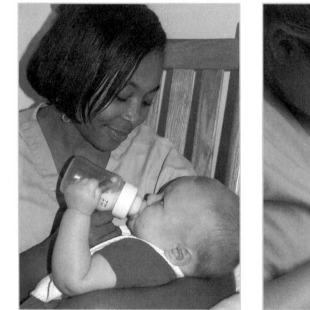 

◆ Refresh, Replenish, and Relax

Do something nice for yourself. Try the caregivers' three Rs—**R**efresh, **R**eplenish, and **R**elax. In order to take care of others, you have to take care of yourself. The bottom line is that to nurture others you need to stay healthy physically, emotionally, mentally, and spiritually. Develop daily habits that are important to your health. Here are some ways to be good to yourself:

- Turn on your favorite music while taking a nice bubble bath.
- Take a relaxing walk in the park.
- Go to the movies with a friend.
- Get lost in a book.
- Do something playful (for example, play a game of hopscotch or jump rope).
- Go out to dinner with your favorite friend.
- Do some physical exercise or join a dance class.
- Try something creative with your hands (for example, a pottery class).
- Learn relaxation techniques like yoga.
- Take a fun and interesting course that may not even be related to children.
- Express yourself through a hobby.

How you take care of yourself is directly linked to how long you can enjoy your profession. To take care of babies you need to take care of yourself, so remember to stay refreshed, replenished, and relaxed.

Key Point

Nurturing yourself is essential to nurturing babies. Caregivers who maintain their emotional and physical well-being are less likely to experience burnout.

Solutions

- Find ways to pamper yourself.
- Realize your ability to nurture babies is affected by the way you nurture yourself.
- Identity and express your feelings in positive ways.
- Use positive communication that creates better working relationships with coworkers.
- Include fun in your life.
- Vent with a friend you can trust.

Chapter 36

Building Team Spirit

Issue

The enjoyment of working with babies is partially influenced by how you relate to your coworkers. Being a part of a team and building team spirit makes you happier at work.

Rationale

How you function in a team, including how you talk with others, can support or undermine the effectiveness of the team. Using strategies that build team spirit and address stumbling blocks that weaken team spirit will result in a stronger sense of community.

Goals

- ◆ To know how you approach and respond to the needs of coworkers and supervisors
- ◆ To use "building blocks" to create team spirit
- ◆ To be a positive force in the team-building process
- ◆ To consider changing a "must do" job into a "want to do" daily experience

How do you work with other team members? Do you prefer to discuss, divide, and share daily tasks at work, or do you prefer to have designated and assigned responsibilities? Are you sensitive in observing when coworkers may need your help? Do you respond as the need arises? How you relate to others at work may make the difference in your general attitude about your job. The relationships you form and develop at your work influence how you feel when you are at work. How much you enjoy being at your job will determine how long you are able to stay in your career.

Doing your job often relies on getting along with coworkers. Issues relating to communication, personalities, leadership, and resources all affect how you feel when at work and how you function in your tasks. For instance, when there is a lack of responsible leadership along with inadequate resources, confusion occurs. When leadership is on shaky ground, it provides a fertile bed for gossip, chaos, and dissatisfaction. Dissatisfaction is a deadly poison to team spirit.

Like many who work in center-based care with babies, some days are better than others. On those good days, team spirit is easy to achieve. On more difficult days, extra effort may be needed to keep the team afloat. For a team to work its best, the entire staff must commit to work together.

Christina, the lead infant caregiver; was watching Tamera, a fairly new caregiver, feed Ally, a 12-month-old infant. Tamera had placed Ally on a stool at a small table. Christina noticed that Tamera was not paying much attention to Ally while she ate. She missed valuable clues about Ally's preferences during eating. At one point, Christina noted Tamera holding the baby's arm and trying to force her to remain on her stool and eat her pears. Ally kept trying to escape off the stool and away from Tamera—a definite struggle.

Christina wanted to go over and "rescue" Ally from the situation Tamera created. She also had thoughts about confronting Tamera's about forcing Ally to stay on the stool. Christina knew the other caregivers in the room were watching to see how she decided to handle the situation. Christina planned to ask Tamera to notice and think what Ally might be saying by her behavior. She waited for Tamera to finish with Ally before taking her aside privately. Christina began by asking, "How do you think you did with feeding Ally?" and proceeded with asking Tamera to describe Ally's reactions to Tamera's caregiving. Through patient unraveling of the event, Tamera was able to understand that she could have been more sensitive to Ally's desire during the feeding process.

Christina supported Tamera by asking her to examine and reflect on how her behavior affected baby Ally. This gave Tamera new insight about how she could respond more sensitively to Ally's cues in the future. Supporting staff members to relate with babies in more responsive ways requires the supervisor to find positive ways of communicating that can help the person change how they provide the care. In this case, if Christina had confronted Tamera and made her feel defensive, Tamera would not have been able to hear the important message of what she could do differently to be more responsive to Ally. Her embarrassment might have caused further problems and feelings of resentment and worthlessness. When Christina supported rather than demoralized Tamera, she was able to be part of the solution for both Tamera and Ally. Tamera had a positive experience with the person she answers to. By being a part of the solution, Christina was able to avoid further problems and hard feelings from her staff members. The person who is in charge of the direction and day-to-day operation of the center has an obligation to staff members. This responsibility includes guiding its members and providing opportunities for positive learning and communication. This fosters respect for each other and understanding, which is necessary for team spirit to flourish.

Two cardinal rules that support team efforts are
◆ Be part of the solution instead of part of the problem.
◆ A little help when needed offsets more difficult problems later on.

When Magda Gerber was teaching professionals about understanding babies, she would often refer to an old Hungarian saying:
> "For every problem under the sun
> There is a solution or there is none.
> If there is one try to find it,
> If there is none never mind it."

This saying reminds us that when you can help, you need to be available, but when the situation is impossible, let it go and put your efforts elsewhere.

Understanding your abilities and limitations in certain situations is the first step in caring about and supporting your coworkers. When coworkers are available to help each other, it is easier to find solutions to problems, resulting in a boost in overall morale. When the staff at a center support each other, a caring atmosphere develops, which helps the team to bond. This bond discourages negative aspects, including feeling isolated and gossiping in the work setting. However, when team spirit is lacking, backbiting, gossiping, and other negative behaviors become the norm. When gossip rules, suspicion flourishes and prevents good programs from succeeding. Below are a list of building blocks and stumbling blocks to team building.

When coworkers are available to help each other, it is easier to find solutions to problems.

◆ Building Blocks to Developing Team Spirit

- ◆ Be responsible about doing your job.
- ◆ Maintain a positive attitude.
- ◆ Deal with problems that arise in constructive ways.
- ◆ Share information with the appropriate person(s).
- ◆ Communicate clearly and concisely.
- ◆ Listen actively to others.
- ◆ State what you mean in respectful ways.
- ◆ Do what you say you will do (keep your promises).
- ◆ Help coworkers when possible.
- ◆ Acknowledge each other's efforts.
- ◆ Celebrate together; smile and enjoy your work.
- ◆ Keep a sense of humor.

◆ Stumbling Blocks to Building Team Spirit

- ◆ Lack of clearly defined roles and responsibilities
- ◆ Unclear house rules or rigid rules and roles
- ◆ Lack of appreciation for one another
- ◆ Lack of supervision, teaming, and administration
- ◆ Lack of possibility for advancement or professional growth dissatisfaction, leading to departures
- ◆ Poor working conditions with few benefits for employees
- ◆ Lack of professional recognition or celebrations of accomplishments
- ◆ Disrespectful behaviors toward one another
- ◆ Poor lines of communication
- ◆ Bringing personal problems to the workplace, which interferes with work
- ◆ Poor attitude about job responsibilities and toward coworkers
- ◆ Tardiness
- ◆ Taking advantage of privileges (for example, frequent use of phone break)

The main difference between work and play is the difference between "want to" and "have to." The key is to work at what it is you want to do, what you enjoy doing.

Most caregivers are at their jobs eight hours a day, five days a week. Because of this, it is important to enjoy what you do and appreciate the people you work with. The main difference between work and play is the difference between "want to" and "have to." Most people view work as "have to" and play as "want to." The key is to work at what it is you want to do, what you enjoy doing. In a way, the goal is to have work be your play. When you work only because you have to, work can become drudgery. Magda Gerber illustrated this in her talk with professionals and parents when she relayed the story of a European gentleman who avidly played tennis several times a day for the sheer pleasure and enjoyment of the sport. He loved playing tennis so much and played so often that it was hard for him to find people to play with. After the Second World War, this same man had lost his money and fortune. He did not have a skill by which to support himself, so he decided to teach tennis lessons. Can you guess what happened to him? The more he taught tennis and the more he *had* to give tennis lessons, the less he enjoyed playing the game. Tennis became a "have to" instead of a "want to." It became drudgery to him, and he lost the enjoyment of the game.

When you enjoy what you do, your work is more satisfying and pleasurable. The effect can be energizing for you and your team. When you enjoy what you do, your work is more rewarding. It is much easier to be a positive team member and help in building a sense of community with your coworkers. A team is a group of people who can rely on each other. Remember, in a team, **t**ogether **e**veryone **a**ccomplishes **m**ore.

Below are a few things to consider that might help you apply some of the information and thoughts in this chapter to your work and your workplace:
- Name one reoccurring problem you have seen in your workplace.
- How did you handle this problem?
- Would you handle this problem differently now?

How would you address the following situation? You are the team manager of three other infant caregivers. You notice they come in late, take advantage of the phone, and grumble about their work situation. Suggest a plan of action that deals with this negative situation and offers positive solutions.

Key Point

Being a part of a team provides you with an opportunity to build team spirit, which, in turn, contributes to work satisfaction.

Solutions

- Be a positive force in team-building efforts.
- Curb behavior that undermines team spirit.
- Consider ways to make your job a more pleasurable work experience.
- Identify a reoccurring problem and find a solution to it.
- Implement respectful ways to help others be more responsive in their care process.

Reflections

Caregiving: A Journey

Where are you in your understanding of babies? Have your observations and experiences with babies given you a different or more expansive insight? Maybe you have found that babies are not totally helpless and have a capacity to participate and be involved in what is happening to them, based on their readiness and development. Maybe you have seen the benefit babies gain by talking with them and telling them what you are doing before you do it. Maybe you have derived pleasure from collaborating in your relationship with babies. It could be that your insights and experiences are beginning to affect your beliefs and actions. Like any journey, there are pitfalls and detours. There are times when you may become distracted or sidetracked. Often it will be exhausting, but journeys can be exciting. They can expand insights as well as provide pleasurable adventures. In truth, journeys often take us down many different roadways as we discover, explore, and investigate life's events.

The journey toward understanding infants is a long one with many varied paths and roads to choose. Some roads may be easier than others. The hard part in this journey lies within us. You may need to explore and discover who you are as a person in order to be effective with babies.

Neisy, an infant caregiver, confided in the lead teacher that when she first began working with babies she did not believe that babies were aware of or able to understand what was happening to them during routine caregiving times. "I really thought it was a bunch of bologna to give the baby so many cues about what I was doing. It kind of felt awkward, and at times, I felt a little foolish," Neisy stated. As she worked with the babies on a daily basis, she began to see and experience their responses to her. "It was amazing to watch babies interact with me about what was happening between us. I didn't believe until then that babies had that capacity to comprehend."

This new experience helped Neisy to appreciate that babies can communicate and respond to what is happening. Until Neisy was open and willing to observe these babies' responses, they would have gone unnoticed, and Neisy would have clung to her old beliefs that babies can't contribute and respond in meaningful ways.

By observing each baby you will learn to understand his or her individual needs and abilities.

Neisy now considers each baby's ability in her caregiving because she understands the value of each baby's involvement. As caregivers, you are asked to identify and acknowledge individual differences in yourself and the babies. There will be times you will have to modify your wishes, responses, and reactions with babies in order to be a more sensitive caregiver. To provide responsive caregiving and stay in touch with babies you must tune in to yourself. As you reflect on yourself and your work with babies, you develop more insight and consciousness about what babies can do. It becomes harder to do mindless caregiving when you expand your understanding of babies.

To embrace insights about babies you need to be open. Observe and think about what you are doing. Your observations and experiences will tell you that each baby is an individual with specific needs and abilities.

When you believe that the active participation by babies is valuable in the relationships you have with babies, you are more likely to give time for their involvement. Over time, the message to the baby is that he or she is respected and valued, which will build his or her self-confidence.

Ann, an infant caregiver, moves to seven-month-old Chloe's crib and asks, "Are you ready to get out of bed?" As Ann does this, she extends her hands toward the baby. Chloe responds by kicking in excitement, and then Ann reaches for Chloe.

When Ann held out her arms and asked Chloe if she would like to get out of the crib, Ann acknowledged that Chloe is an individual with choices and preferences. She may or may not want to get out of her bed at that particular time. By giving Chloe the time to respond, Ann is including Chloe's choice and preference in the caregiving process. This simple act empowers Chloe as a beginning decision-maker.

The philosophy of being actively involved with the baby allows mutual cooperation to develop between you and the baby. As you and the baby relate to each other in tuned-in ways, sensitive caregiving flourishes. This allows the baby to be more satisfied and understood. You can also begin to understand how your thoughts, feelings, and beliefs about babies affect the care process. The care you give babies affects their attitudes about themselves. Identifying and reflecting about your feelings helps to monitor your behavior with babies. Reflecting on experiences with babies takes a commitment that is worthwhile.

The care you give babies affects their attitudes about themselves.

The following tool has been designed to help you reflect on your feelings and experiences. This tool is a road map in your travel toward understanding infants. It will help you look at where you are, where you have been, and where you want to go in your journey with babies. One way to use this tool is to write the answers in a journal and review and reflect on the questions every month. Keeping a monthly log of your answers to these reflective questions can help you to monitor any changes in your thoughts, attitudes, and actions.

◆ Road Map to Understanding Infants

1. What is one belief you had about babies?
2. How did the belief affect your attitude about babies?
3. What is now the most important belief you have about babies?
4. What influenced the change in your belief about babies?
5. Give an example of how you recently showed respect while caring for a baby.
6. Describe your initial feelings when you hear a baby cry.
7. In observing babies, what one thing surprised you?
8. How do you show you value babies as individuals?

When you work with babies, you gain new insights about babies and yourself. Rereading your answers to the above questions and comments six months from now will let you know if any changes have occurred in your thoughts, attitudes, and actions. Each caregiver designs his or her own professional journey. Your thoughts, responses, and emotions influence the health and well-being of the babies in your care. Could you ask for a better way to make a lasting contribution to society?

◆ A Note from the Authors

We hope this book has given you meaningful ways to approach babies in your care. Our thoughts in these chapters are meant to support and guide you in your journey toward understanding babies and understanding how your relationship can be filled with rich and meaningful experiences for both you and the babies in your care. We believe that you are the most valuable resource for babies to thrive in group care. It is our hope that you also believe you make a difference in babies through the day-to-day experiences that you have with them.

As a caregiver, you make a difference in how well the babies in your care thrive.

References and Resources

Bayer, C. L., Whaley, K. L., & May, S. F. 1995. Strategic assistance in toddler disputes: II. Sequences and patterns of teachers' message strategies. Special Issue: Conflict resolution in early social development. *Early Education & Development, 6,* 405–432.

Berk, L. E. 2005. *Infants and children: Prenatal through middle childhood.* 5th ed. Boston: Pearson Education, Inc.

Bettelheim, B. 1987. *A good enough parent: The guide to bringing up children.* New York: Knopf.

Bredekamp, S., & Copple, C. (Eds.). 1997. *Developmentally appropriate practice in early childhood programs.* Revised ed. Washington, DC: NAEYC.

Caulfield, R. 1995. Reciprocity between infants and caregivers during the first year of life. *Early Childhood Education 23*(1), 3–7.

Coles, R. 1997. *The moral intelligence of children: How to raise a moral child.* New York: Plume.

Da Ros, D. A., & Kovach, B. A. 1998. Toddlers and caregivers during conflict. *Childhood Education 75*(1), 25–30.

DeVries, R., & Zan, B. 1996. A constructivist perspective on the role of the sociomoral atmosphere in promoting children's development. In C. T. Fosnet (Ed.), *Constructivism: Theory, perspectives, and practice* (pp. 103–119). New York: Teachers College Press.

Dewar, J. (Quotes in L. Adams & P. Kostell, Eds.) 1998. *Quotations for early childhood Educators* (p. 40). Olney, MD: Association for Childhood Education International.

Eisler, R. 2007. *The real wealth of nations: Creating a caring economics.* San Francisco: Berrett-Koehler Publishers.

Elliot, E. 2003. Helping a baby adjust to center care. *Young Children 58*(4), 22–28.

Gerber, M. (Ed.). 1979. *A manual for parents and professionals.* Los Angeles: Resources for Infant Educarers.

Gerber, M. 1978. *On their own with our help.* Video available from Resources for Infant Educarers, 1550 Murray Circle, Los Angeles, CA 90026.

Gerber, M. 1998. *Dear parent: Caring for infants with respect* (2nd ed.; J. Weaver, Ed.). Los Angeles: Resources for Infant Educarers.

Gerber, M., & Johnson, A. 1998. *Your self-confident baby: How to encourage your child's natural abilities—from the very start.* New York: Wiley.

Gonzalez-Mena, J., & Eyer, D. W. 2004. *Infants, toddlers, and caregivers: A curriculum of respectful, responsive care and education* (6th ed.). Boston: McGraw Hill.

Honig, A. S. 2002. *Secure relationships: Nurturing infant/toddler attachment in early care settings.* Washington, DC: NAEYC.

Honig, A. S., & Lally, R. J. 1988. Behavior profiles of experienced teachers of infants and toddlers. *Early Childhood Development and Care 33*(1–4), 181–199.

Howes, C. 1998, June/July. *Continuity of care: The importance of infant-toddler caregiver relationships.* Washington, DC: Zero to Three.

Kallo, E., & Balog, G. 2005. *The origins of free play.* Budapest, Hungary: Pickler-Loczy Tarsasag.

Kovach, B. A., & Da Ros, D. A. 1995. The use of language: A rationale for respectful and reciprocal caregiving with infants. *Montessori Life 7*(2), 16–17.

Kovach, B. A., & Da Ros, D. A. 1998. Respectful, individual, and responsive caregiving for infants: the key to successful care in group settings. *Young Children 53*(3), 61–74.

Lally, R. J. 1995. The impact of child care policies and practices on infant/toddler identity formation. *Young Children 51*(1), 58–67.

Lally, R. J., & Mangione, P. 2006. The uniqueness of infancy demands a responsive approach to care. *Young Children 61*(4), 14–20.

Lally, J. R., Griffin, A., Fenichel, E., Segal, M., Szanton, E., & Weissbourd, B. 1995. *Caring for infants and toddlers in groups.* Washington, DC: Zero to Three.

National Scientific Council of the Developing Child. 2004. *Young children develop in an environment of relationships (working paper no. 1).* Washington, DC: Author. Available online www.Developingchild.net/pubs/wp/Young_Children_Environmental_Relationships.pdf

Piaget, J. 1965/1932. *The moral judgment of the child.* London: Free Press.

Pikler, E. 1969. *Data on gross-motor development of the infant.* Budapest, Hungary: Publishing House of the Hungarian Academy of Science.

Pikler, E. 1978. The competence of the infant. *Acte Paediatrica Academiae Scientiarum Hungaricae, 20,* 185–192.

Rogers, F. M. 1998. *Opening general session.* Presentation at the National Association for the Education of Young Children, Toronto, Canada.

Tizard, B., Cooperman, O., Joseph, A. & Tizard, J. 1972. Environmental effects on language development: A study of young children in long-stay Residential nurseries. *Child Development, 4,* 337–358.

Zero to Three, National Center for Infants, Toddlers, & Families. 1995. *Caring for infants and toddlers in groups: Developmentally appropriate practice.* Arlington, VA: Author.

Appendix

Developmental Chart

Sample Floor Plan

Daily Observation Form

Developmental Characteristics of Babies 1 month to 18 months

	1–4 months	4–8 months
Physical	• Moves from reflex to more purposeful movement • Holds head up • Moves from side to side • May roll over • Studies hands • Brings objects to mouth • Reaches for objects	• Moves intentionally • Begins to develop eye-hand coordination • Discovers feet • Rolls onto stomach from back and from back to stomach • Moves toward what he or she sees and hears • May sit up or crawl • Transfers objects from hand to hand
Cognitive	• Visually tracks an object • Shows a preference for a family member—able to recognize who and what belongs in the environment • Looks at the mouth of person speaking • Gazes at objects • Curious—shows interest in environment	• Distinguishes different properties of objects • Finds hidden objects • Solves simple problems • Holds the idea of something in his or her brain (object permanence) • Repeats actions • Moves intentionally
Social-Emotional	• Laughs socially • Smiles interactively • Responds to familiar voices • Smiles after recognizing someone • Is responsive to attention	• Explores his or her environment • Initiates social interactions • Develops stranger anxiety • Shows resistance—begins to develop his or her will • Has goal-directed behaviors • Expresses emotions (happy, sad, anxious, and so on) • Smiles broadly • Looks for reactions on the faces of others
Language	• Coos • Makes "raspberries" • Makes sounds	• Babbles • May say "ma ma" or "da da" • Develops more selective hearing • Understands gestures • Starts to communicate with other infants or shows interest in doing so

Developmental Characteristics of Babies 1 month to 18 months

8–12 months	12–18 months	
• Creeps • Sits up • Stoops • Pivots • Pulls up, cruises • May walk • Grasps objects of choice and releases them • Dumps • Throws	• Walks alone • Explores his or her environment • Climbs • Opens and closes objects • Uses tools, such as a spoon • Carries objects when walking • Uses a pincer grip	**Physical**
• Recognizes his or her name and the names of familiar objects • Has memory—begins to remember people, events, and objects • Holds a concept in his or her mind • Thinks symbolically • Has comprehension—begins to understand simple commands, a few words, and body gestures • Understands two- and three-word sentences • Acts intentionally	• Loves opposites • Identifies objects and pictures • Practices trial and error • Repeats actions • Understands that objects have names • Is interested in cause and effect • Responds to commands or requests • Returns to activity of interest	**Cognitive**
• Anticipates activities • Is emotionally expressive • Anticipates the return of his or her mother, father • Plays more interactively with others (peek-a-boo)	• Is enthusiastic • Shows excitement and elation • Loves an audience • Begins to hold back anger • Insists on his or her own way • Is a watchful observer • Is very interested in peers	**Social-Emotional**
• Begins to understand that words have meaning • Says first intentional word • Imitates sounds and vocalizations • Demonstrates symbolic hand gestures	• May say "please" • Mimics actions • Names objects • Repeats animal sounds • May use some words to communicate • Absorbs language and tries to communicate	**Language**

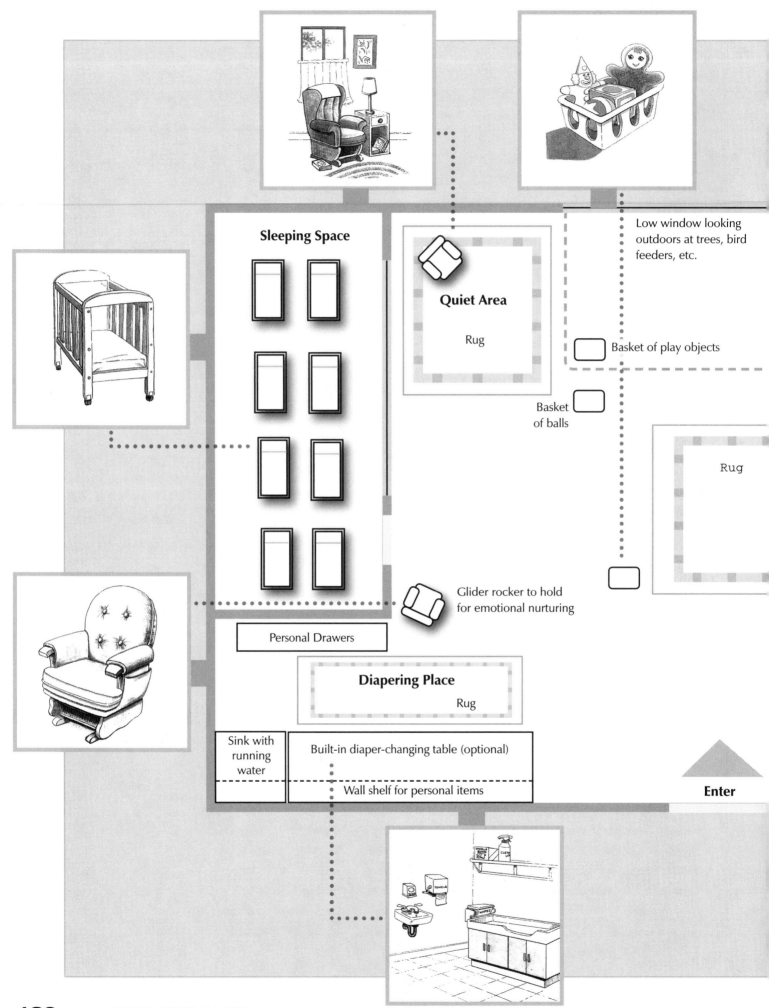

Sleeping Space

Quiet Area

Rug

Low window looking outdoors at trees, bird feeders, etc.

Basket of play objects

Basket of balls

Rug

Glider rocker to hold for emotional nurturing

Personal Drawers

Diapering Place

Rug

Sink with running water	Built-in diaper-changing table (optional)
	Wall shelf for personal items

Enter

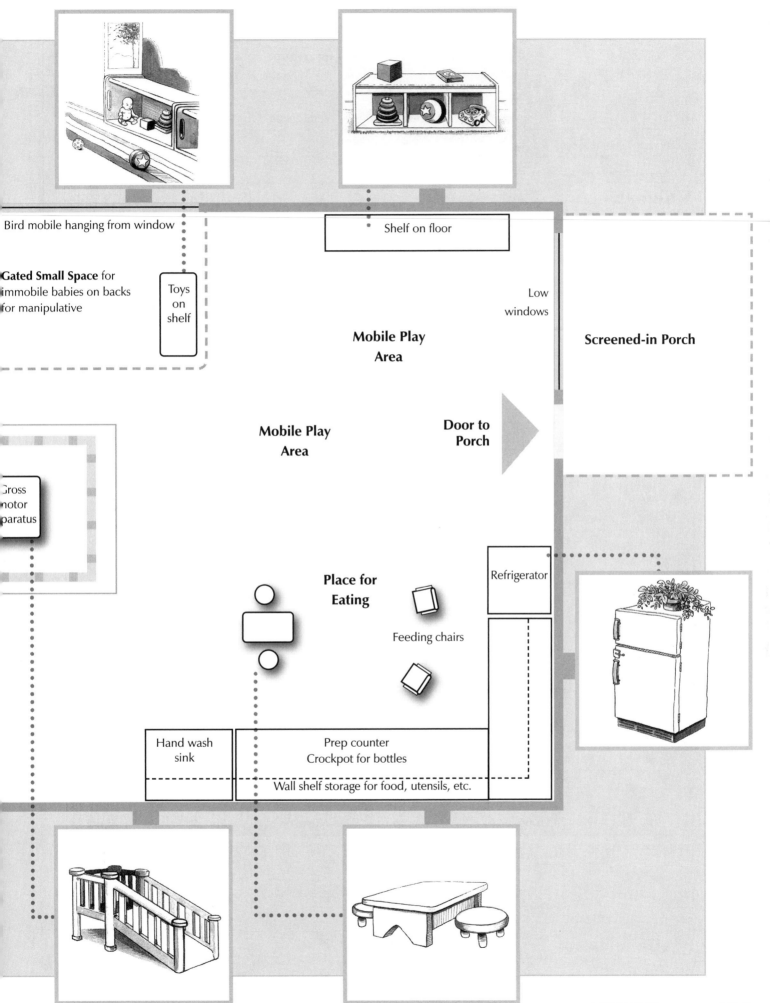

Bird mobile hanging from window

Gated Small Space for immobile babies on backs for manipulative

Toys on shelf

Shelf on floor

Low windows

Mobile Play Area

Screened-in Porch

Gross motor apparatus

Mobile Play Area

Door to Porch

Place for Eating

Feeding chairs

Refrigerator

Hand wash sink

Prep counter
Crockpot for bottles

Wall shelf storage for food, utensils, etc.

Daily Observation Form

Name: _____ Week of: _____

	Monday		Tuesday		Wednesday		Thursday		Friday	
Parents' Comments										
Arrival Time										
Last Fed (amount)										
Awake Time										
Diapering	Wet	BM	Wet	BM	Wet	BM	Wet	BM	Wet	BM
7 am–9 am										
9 am–11 am										
11 am–1 pm										
1 pm–3 pm										
Eating	Time	Amount	Time	Amount	Time	Amount	Time	Amount	Time	Amount
Fluids										
Snack	Time		Time		Time		Time		Time	
Lunch	Time		Time		Time		Time		Time	
Snack	Time		Time		Time		Time		Time	
Sleeping	Sleep	Awake	Sleep	Awake	Sleep	Awake	Sleep	Awake	Sleep	Awake

Observation Activities

Social	Emotional	Language	Manipulative	Gross Motor	Outdoor

Additional Comments _____

_____

Index

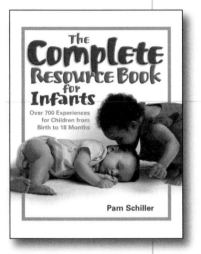

Gryphon House | 19223
ISBN 978-0-87659-295-3

The Complete Resource Book for Infants
Over 700 Experiences for Children from Birth to 18 Months
Pam Schiller

The third in the best-selling *Complete Resource* series, *The Complete Resource Book for Infants* features more than 700 experiences and activities that are perfect for infants from birth through 18 months. The ideas are organized by developmental area: language, social-emotional, physical, and cognitive, which are the essential building blocks of infant development. The appendix is chock-full of songs, rhymes, recipes, sign language, recommended books and toys, and family connection resources. 272 pages. 2005.

Gryphon House | 16927
ISBN 978-0-87659-287-8

The Complete Resource Book for Toddlers and Twos
Over 2000 Experiences and Ideas
Pam Schiller

Best-selling author Pam Schiller offers learning experiences that focus on the prime areas of development for toddlers and twos. Easy to implement, each of the 100 daily topics is divided into activities and experiences that support language enrichment, cognitive development, social-emotional development, and physical development. A detailed appendix offers a quick, easy reference to helpful tools such as craft patterns, flannel storyboards, sign language diagrams, and reproducible letters home. Teachers will be delighted to add the ideas in this generous resource to their current lesson plans. 576 pages. 2003.

The Infant/Toddler Photo Activity Library
An Essential Literacy Tool
Pam Schiller

This essential teaching tool helps caregivers and parents develop language and literacy skills with infants and toddlers. The sturdy four-color photo cards are organized by theme. Each card has a photograph of people or objects that infants and toddlers encounter every day. The back of each photo card has a vocabulary list, suggested activities for each photograph, the American Sign Language sign related to the image, and a recommended children's book. Compatible with any program, this indispensable tool will be invaluable for infant and toddler caregivers. It comes in its own carrying pouch with dividers for organizing the cards by theme. 52 photo cards (9" x 12").

Gryphon House | 17632
ISBN 978-0-87659-034-8

Story S-t-r-e-t-c-h-e-r-s® for Infants, Toddlers, and Twos
Experiences, Activities, and Games for Popular Children's Books
Shirley Raines, Karen Miller, and Leah Curry-Rood

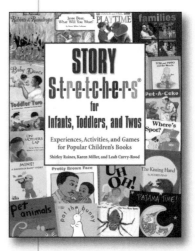

Story S-t-r-e-t-c-h-e-r-s® for Infants, Toddlers, and Twos contains suggestions for more than 100 age-appropriate children's books and 240 ideas for expanding stories in new ways to enhance the learning process. Organized by age, this book is a wonderful addition to the *Story S-t-r-e-t-c-h-e-r-s®* series, offering new ways for young children to experience the magic of a good book. Children reap amazing benefits from being exposed to reading at an early age, and *Story S-t-r-e-t-c-h-e-r-s® for Infants, Toddlers, and Twos* makes reading an adventure in learning and fun! 192 pages. 2002.

★ *Early Childhood News Directors' Choice Award*

Gryphon House |18931
ISBN 978-0-87659-274-8

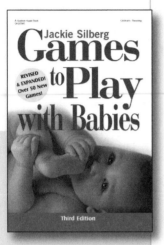

Gryphon House | 16285
ISBN 978-0-87659-255-7

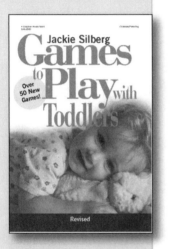

Gryphon House | 19587
ISBN 978-0-87659-234-2

Gryphon House | 12687
ISBN 978-0-87659-235-9

Games to Play with Babies, Third Edition
Jackie Silberg

Hundreds of games to play with your baby to encourage bonding, coordination, motor skills, and more! This indispensable book shows you how to build important developmental skills while enjoying time with your baby. Use these everyday activities to nurture and stimulate self-confidence, coordination, social skills, and much, much more. Give your baby a great start with this wonderful collection of over 225 fun-filled games! 256 pages. 2001.

★ Ben Franklin Award, finalist in Parenting
★ National Parenting Press Award
★ Parent's Guide to Children's Media Award

Games to Play with Toddlers, Revised
Jackie Silberg

Revised and updated with all-new illustrations and over 200 games, this indispensable book helps you develop areas important for the growth of your 12- to 24-month-old—areas such as language, creativity, coordination, confidence, problem-solving, and gross-motor skills. You and your toddler will experience the joy of discovery on every fun-filled page! 256 pages. 2002.

★ Parent Choice Awards
★ Parent's Guide to Children's Media Award

Games to Play with Two Year Olds, Revised
Jackie Silberg

Revised and updated, *Games to Play with Two Year Olds* is packed with opportunities to build confidence and to enhance language, coordination, social interactions, and problem-solving skills. *Games to Play with Two Year Olds* is a must-have for anyone caring for a child between the ages of 2 and 3. Turn ordinary, everyday routines into fun learning experiences! 256 pages. 2002.

★ Parent Council Award
★ National Parenting Press Award
★ *Early Childhood News* Directors' Choice Award

Simple Transitions for Infants and Toddlers

Karen Miller

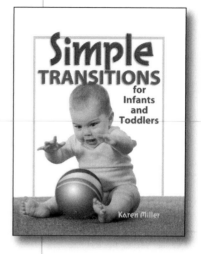

Have you ever had trouble getting an infant to settle down for her nap, or persuading a group of toddlers to pick up their toys? If so, this book is for you! *Simple Transitions*, a must-have resource for teachers who work with the youngest age group. It offers more than 400 tips, ideas, and easy-to-do activities from an expert in the infant/toddler field. There are even ideas to help parents deal with the bigger transitions in their children's lives, such as separation anxiety and toilet learning. *Simple Transitions* is an indispensable book for teachers of infants and toddlers! 176 pages. 2004.

★ *Early Childhood News Directors' Choice Award*

Gryphon House | 12134
ISBN 978-0-87659-298-4

The Complete Learning Spaces Book for Infants and Toddlers
54 Integrated Areas with Play Experiences

Rebecca Isbell and Christy Isbell

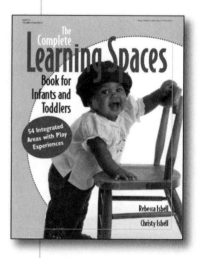

Fill your classroom with playful learning spaces specially designed for infants and toddlers with these easy-to-implement ideas. This comprehensive book includes ideas for planning, using, and evaluating age-appropriate learning spaces, such as "I See," "I Move," and "I Hear." Information for each learning space is complete with detailed illustrations, learning objectives, lists of props, age-appropriate activities, literacy connections, and vocabulary lists. This book is essential for every infant and toddler program. 400 pages. 2004.

★ Association of Educational Publishers' Distinguished
   Achievment Award, Finalist

Gryphon House | 16917
ISBN 978-0-87659-293-9